55 WITCHES

55 Short Stories from the
Life of Witches

Moneta Agency

Copyright © 2023 Moneta Agency

All rights reserved

The characters and events portrayed in this book are fictitious. Any similarity to real persons, living or dead, is coincidental and not intended by the author.

No part of this book may be reproduced, or stored in a retrieval system, or transmitted in any form or by any means, electronic, mechanical, photocopying, recording, or otherwise, without express written permission of the publisher.

ISBN: 9798388085665

Cover design by: Moneta Agency
Library of Congress Control Number: 2018675309
Printed in the United States of America

CONTENTS

Title Page
Copyright
About Publishing House
Introduction

1 Self-Love and Resilience	1
2 Journey to Clarity and Purpose	5
3 Self-Care and Inner Harmony	9
4 Magical Mastery and the Power of Positive Habits	13
5 Self-Love and Radical Acceptance	17
6 Life Explorer	21
7 The Solo	25
8 The Simple Things	29
9 Giving Up the Gift	33
10 The Lost Heart	37
11 Fearful	41
12 The Skeptical	45
13 Traveler to Lost Cities	48
14 Self-Healing	52
15 Coping with the Shadows	55
16 Weaving Dreams	58
17 The Rescue	62

18 Knowing the Future	65
19 Walking Through the Walls	69
20 The Gift of Flight	72
21 The Magic Voice	75
22 Just the Way I Want it	79
23 Always a Winner	82
24 The Curious	86
25 Party Girl	89
26 The Lovely	92
27 The Enterprising	95
28 The Selfless	98
29 Altering the Past	101
30 The Scandalist	105
31 The Anxious	108
32 The Indecisive	111
33 Forever Young	114
34 The Fear of Loss	118
35 The Lonely	121
36 Speaking to the Winds	124
37 Waiting for Salvation	128
38 The Immortal	131
39 Mother's Daughter	134
40 The Lost	138
41 The Mother Bird	141
42 The Phony	144
43 A Seeker of Vivid Impressions	148
44 The Wrong	151
45 The Forgotten Name	154

46 The Defender	158
47 The World Changer	161
48 The Spotlighted	164
49 Roses Against the Wind	168
50 The Healing Food	171
51 The Stubborn Heart	174
52 The Suspicious	178
53 Forgotten Way into the Dream World	182
54 The Mysterious and Deceptive Signs	186
55 The Creative	191
No Number Story) The Universal Dance	195
Conclusion	199
Leave the Rewiev	212

ABOUT PUBLISHING HOUSE

Welcome to Moneta Agency, where our authors are given the freedom to express themselves openly and sincerely without fear of judgment or repercussion. Our agency provides a safe and secure space for writers who wish to remain anonymous, allowing them to share their thoughts and ideas without compromising their social status or personal relationships.

At our agency, we understand that sometimes the most honest and powerful writing comes from those who choose to remain anonymous. Whether it be due to personal or professional reasons, our authors are able to write with complete freedom and authenticity without any concern for how others may perceive their work.

Our mission is to support these writers and help them share their stories with the world. We believe that everyone should have the opportunity to express themselves creatively without fear of censorship or reprisal.

Our publishing process is completely confidential, and we work closely with our authors to ensure their anonymity is always protected. We pride ourselves on our dedication to professionalism, and we treat every author with the utmost respect and sensitivity.

We publish a wide range of genres, including fiction, non-fiction, poetry, and memoirs, and our books are available in a variety of formats, including e-books, print books, and audiobooks. We are dedicated to ensuring that our authors' voices are heard, and we work tirelessly to promote their work to a wide audience.

Thank you for considering our publishing agency, where anonymity meets creativity and where the power of words can change lives.

INTRODUCTION

All stories want to be told and preferably many times. So they are always on the lookout for someone to live with them. Once a lucky man is found, the story penetrates his whole being and engages him in a journey. This book contains 55 stories lived by beautiful, clever, and lucky witches at some point because witches are very receptive to stories. They always sense the approach of new stories and the end of old ones. We hope you enjoy reading these stories, and perhaps some of them will one day want to be lived by you. Read the table of contents first and start with the stories whose title catches your attention. It will be fun, you'll see. Good luck and lots of happiness!

1 SELF-LOVE AND RESILIENCE

Once upon a time, in a quaint little village nestled in the heart of an enchanted forest, there lived a beautiful and cheerful witch named Lila. Lila was known far and wide for her remarkable powers and her unwavering kindness. She had an infectious laugh and could always be seen with a bright smile on her face. Her long, flowing hair was the color of sunshine, and her sparkling green eyes held the warmth of a thousand sunsets.

Lila loved her life and the people in her village, but she harbored a secret that no one knew. For years, she had allowed others to control her actions and decisions, eager to please everyone around her. She constantly sought validation from others, believing that if she could make everyone else happy, she would find happiness herself. She was unaware of the importance of self-love, and so she lived her life to meet the expectations of others.

Over time, the pressure of pleasing everyone else began to take its toll on Lila. Her once cheerful demeanor began to fade, and she found herself sinking deeper and deeper into despair. Her once-bright eyes now held the heavy weight of sadness, and her laughter was lost to the winds.

One day, as Lila sat by a tranquil stream, she noticed a small, delicate flower growing at the water's edge. It was a vibrant shade of purple, and it seemed to radiate with inner light. Intrigued, Lila reached out and touched the flower gently. As she did so, a warm energy enveloped her, and she felt a sudden wave of calm wash over her.

A wise old spirit appeared before her, taking the form of an ancient tree. The spirit, sensing Lila's sorrow, spoke softly, "Dear Lila, why do you carry such a heavy burden in your heart?"

Tears welled up in Lila's eyes as she replied, "I have spent my life trying to make others happy, but I have lost myself in the process. I no longer know who I am or what I want."

The wise spirit nodded gently, understanding Lila's pain. "My dear child, you have forgotten the most important person in your life: yourself. It is time for you to rediscover the love you have within you. Only when you learn to love yourself can you truly shine."

Lila listened to the spirit's words, and as she did so, she began to understand the importance of self-love. She realized that it was not her duty to meet the expectations of others, but rather to live her life in a way that brought her joy and fulfillment. She began to practice showing kindness and grace to herself, regardless of the outcome of her actions.

As Lila embraced her newfound sense of self-love, her inner light began to shine once more. Her laughter returned to the winds, and her eyes sparkled with happiness. She discovered that self-love is what shines through even when we don't achieve our goals or meet our measurements of success. By being kind and gracious to herself, Lila found the strength to stand tall and live a life that was true to her heart.

The villagers noticed the change in Lila and were inspired by her newfound confidence and happiness. They, too, began to learn the importance of self-love, and the village was filled with a warm, loving energy.

And so, Lila the beautiful and cheerful witch continued to share her light with others, helping them discover the power of self-love. The enchanted forest and the village within it thrived, united by the understanding that self-love is the truest form of magic.

55 WITCHES

Close your eyes and still the time around you. Can you feel the story coming alive within you? What do you need to alter to create a new experience? Allow yourself to be enveloped by the possibilities unfurling before you. What will you see? What will you feel in the depths of this new story?

Please write it down or stare at this empty page until it is filled with visions of magic, mystery and transformation.

Enjoy yourself!

2 JOURNEY TO CLARITY AND PURPOSE

Once upon a time, in a magical realm that existed beyond the realm of human understanding, there lived a beautiful, intelligent, and enterprising witch named Aria. Aria was known throughout the realm for her vast knowledge of spells and potions, as well as her incredible ability to create enchanting works of art from the simplest of materials. She had a keen mind for business and was a master of her craft, respected and admired by all who crossed her path.

Despite her many talents and successes, Aria found herself constantly burdened by the weight of her own expectations. She was always worrying about the minutiae of life, unable to let go of what didn't matter and focus on what truly did. As a result, she was often overwhelmed and struggled to find a sense of clarity and purpose in her life.

One fateful day, Aria stumbled upon a mysterious, ancient library nestled deep within the heart of the enchanted forest. Intrigued, she ventured inside, the scent of old parchment and aged leather filling her senses. As she explored the towering shelves, her eyes fell upon a dusty, leather-bound tome. The golden letters on the cover read: "The Book of Clarity."

Feeling drawn to the book, Aria opened it and began to read. The pages revealed long-lost wisdom, guiding her to let go of the unimportant details that clouded her mind and heart. She discovered that the key to finding clarity and purpose was to embrace the present moment and focus on the things that truly mattered to her.

With each word she read, a sense of peace and understanding washed over Aria. She began to apply the wisdom from the book to her everyday life, learning to discern the essential from the trivial. Slowly but surely, she let go of the worries and expectations that had once consumed her thoughts.

As Aria embraced this newfound clarity, she discovered a sense of purpose she had never known before. Her mind was no longer clouded by insignificant matters, allowing her to concentrate on her true passions and desires. She began to create even more extraordinary works of art, her magical abilities enhanced by her clear and focused mind.

Aria also used her knowledge and skills to benefit others, opening a school of magic and art to help young witches and wizards find their own clarity and purpose. Through her teachings, she showed her students the importance of living in the present and focusing on what truly mattered to them.

As the years passed, Aria's reputation grew, and her school became a renowned institution in the magical realm. Witches and wizards from far and wide traveled to learn from her wisdom and experience the transformative power of clarity and purpose.

Aria's life was forever changed by the ancient book she had discovered in that mysterious library. She had found the key to unlocking her full potential and living a life of true fulfillment. And through her teachings, she shared that gift with countless others, helping them find their own sense of clarity and purpose in their magical lives.

55 WITCHES

Close your eyes and still the time around you. Can you feel the story coming alive within you? What do you need to alter to create a new experience? Allow yourself to be enveloped by the possibilities unfurling before you. What will you see? What will you feel in the depths of this new story?

Please write it down or stare at this empty page until it is filled with visions of magic, mystery and transformation.

Enjoy yourself!

3 SELF-CARE AND INNER HARMONY

Once upon a time, in a whimsical village nestled between the rolling hills and a sparkling river, there lived a delightful and fun witch named Elara. Elara was known far and wide for her contagious laughter, her incredible magical skills, and her ability to turn even the dreariest of days into a bright, joyful celebration. She was a beacon of light in the village, and her presence was cherished by all who knew her.

However, unbeknownst to many, Elara's life was not always filled with joy and laughter. Behind her bright facade, she struggled with the weight of toxic energy that drained her spirit and clouded her happiness. She was surrounded by people who did not understand her or appreciate her magical abilities, and their negativity weighed heavily on her heart.

One fateful day, as Elara wandered through the enchanted forest, she stumbled upon a small, hidden glade filled with the most beautiful, fragrant flowers she had ever seen. Intrigued by the serene atmosphere, she decided to sit down and rest among the blossoms.

As she inhaled the sweet aroma of the flowers, Elara felt a gentle warmth envelop her. A soft voice whispered in her ear, "You must learn to care for yourself, dear Elara, to overcome the darkness that surrounds you and find the light within."

In that moment, Elara realized that she had been neglecting her own well-being, allowing the toxic energy around her to dim her inner light. She knew it was time to change her ways and prioritize her own happiness and well-being.

Elara began to practice self-care, dedicating time each day to nurturing her body, mind, and soul. She took long, leisurely walks through the enchanted forest, soaking in the beauty and tranquility of her surroundings. She meditated by the sparkling river, allowing the soothing sound of the water to wash away her worries and stress.

As she took better care of herself, Elara also learned to recognize and avoid the toxic energy that had once burdened her heart. She distanced herself from those who did not support or appreciate her, and instead, she surrounded herself with loving, positive people who encouraged her growth and happiness.

With each day that passed, Elara's inner light grew stronger and brighter. She embraced her magical abilities with newfound confidence and joy, using them to bring happiness and laughter to the village. Her delightful, fun-loving nature became even more infectious, and her presence was like a ray of sunshine that warmed the hearts of all who crossed her path.

Over time, Elara's commitment to self-care and her determination to overcome toxic energy transformed not only her own life but also the lives of those around her. The village flourished under her influence, becoming a place where love, laughter, and well-being were celebrated and cherished.

Elara's story became a testament to the power of self-care and the importance of prioritizing one's own well-being. Through her journey, she discovered that in order to truly shine, one must first learn to nurture the light within.

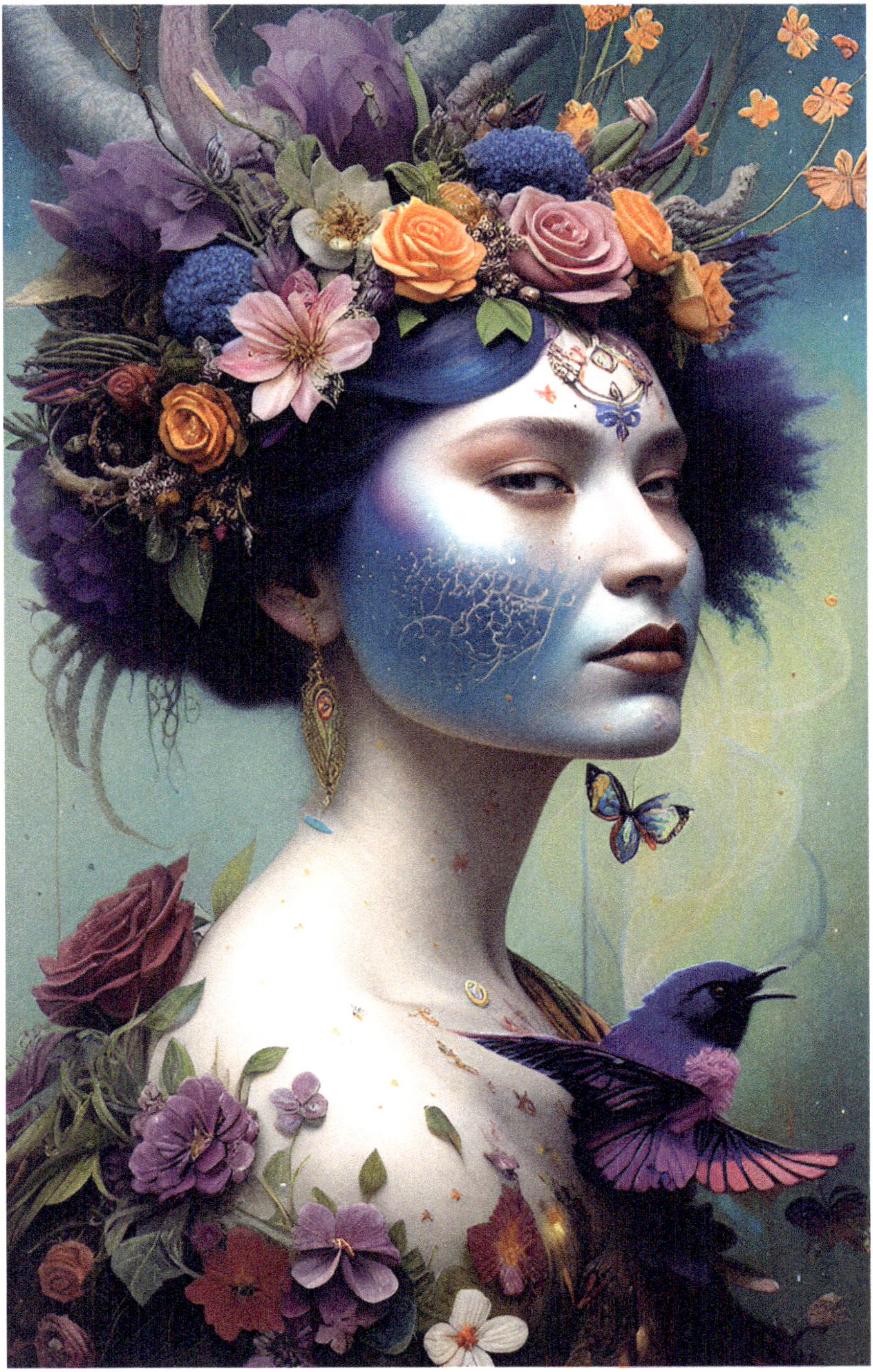

Close your eyes and still the time around you. Can you feel the story coming alive within you? What do you need to alter to create a new experience? Allow yourself to be enveloped by the possibilities unfurling before you. What will you see? What will you feel in the depths of this new story?

Please write it down or stare at this empty page until it is filled with visions of magic, mystery and transformation.

Enjoy yourself!

4 MAGICAL MASTERY AND THE POWER OF POSITIVE HABITS

In a vibrant, bustling city known for its magical wonders and enchanting beauty, there lived an amazing and joyful witch named Selene. Selene was known throughout the city for her incredible mastery of the magical arts and her unrelenting positivity. Despite her many accomplishments, Selene was not always the talented and joyful witch she was renowned to be.

Years ago, Selene struggled with her magical abilities, her self-confidence, and her sense of purpose. She longed to unlock her full potential, but her limiting beliefs held her back, and great opportunities seemed to elude her. Disheartened, she began to question whether she was truly meant to be a powerful witch.

One fateful evening, while wandering through a moonlit garden, Selene encountered a wise, ancient owl perched on a branch overhead. The owl, sensing Selene's inner turmoil, spoke to her in a calm and soothing voice, "Young witch, you hold within you the power to change your life and achieve greatness, but you must first change your beliefs and cultivate positive life habits."

Intrigued and inspired, Selene decided to take the owl's advice to heart. She began a journey of personal growth, learning to replace her limiting beliefs with empowering ones. She practiced affirmations, visualizations, and meditation, allowing her newfound positive beliefs to take root in her mind and heart.

As she changed her beliefs, Selene also developed healthy habits that contributed to her overall well-being and the enhancement of her magical abilities. She rose with the sun each morning, spending time in quiet reflection and setting her intentions for the day. She nourished her body with wholesome, magical foods and exercised regularly to maintain her strength and stamina.

Selene's dedication to cultivating positive life habits also extended to her relationships and surroundings. She surrounded herself with supportive, like-minded individuals who encouraged her growth and celebrated her successes. She fostered an environment of love, kindness, and mutual respect, and in turn, her magical abilities flourished.

As Selene continued to transform her beliefs and habits, she noticed an incredible shift in her life. Opportunities she had once only dreamt of began to manifest before her eyes. Doors opened, and her magical talents grew stronger and more versatile, earning her respect and admiration from her fellow witches and wizards.

With each passing day, Selene's mastery of the magical arts reached new heights. Her once-dim light now shone brighter than ever, illuminating the lives of those around her. Her joy and enthusiasm for life were contagious, inspiring others to embark on their own journeys of self-discovery and personal growth.

Selene's story became a testament to the power of positive beliefs and the impact of cultivating healthy life habits. Through her journey, she demonstrated that greatness lies within each of us, waiting to be unlocked by the choices we make and the beliefs we hold dear.

The city continued to flourish under Selene's influence, as she shared her wisdom and knowledge with those who sought to learn from her experiences. The amazing and joyful witch became a beacon of inspiration, proving that the key to achieving incredible mastery lies in the power of our minds and the habits we choose to embrace.

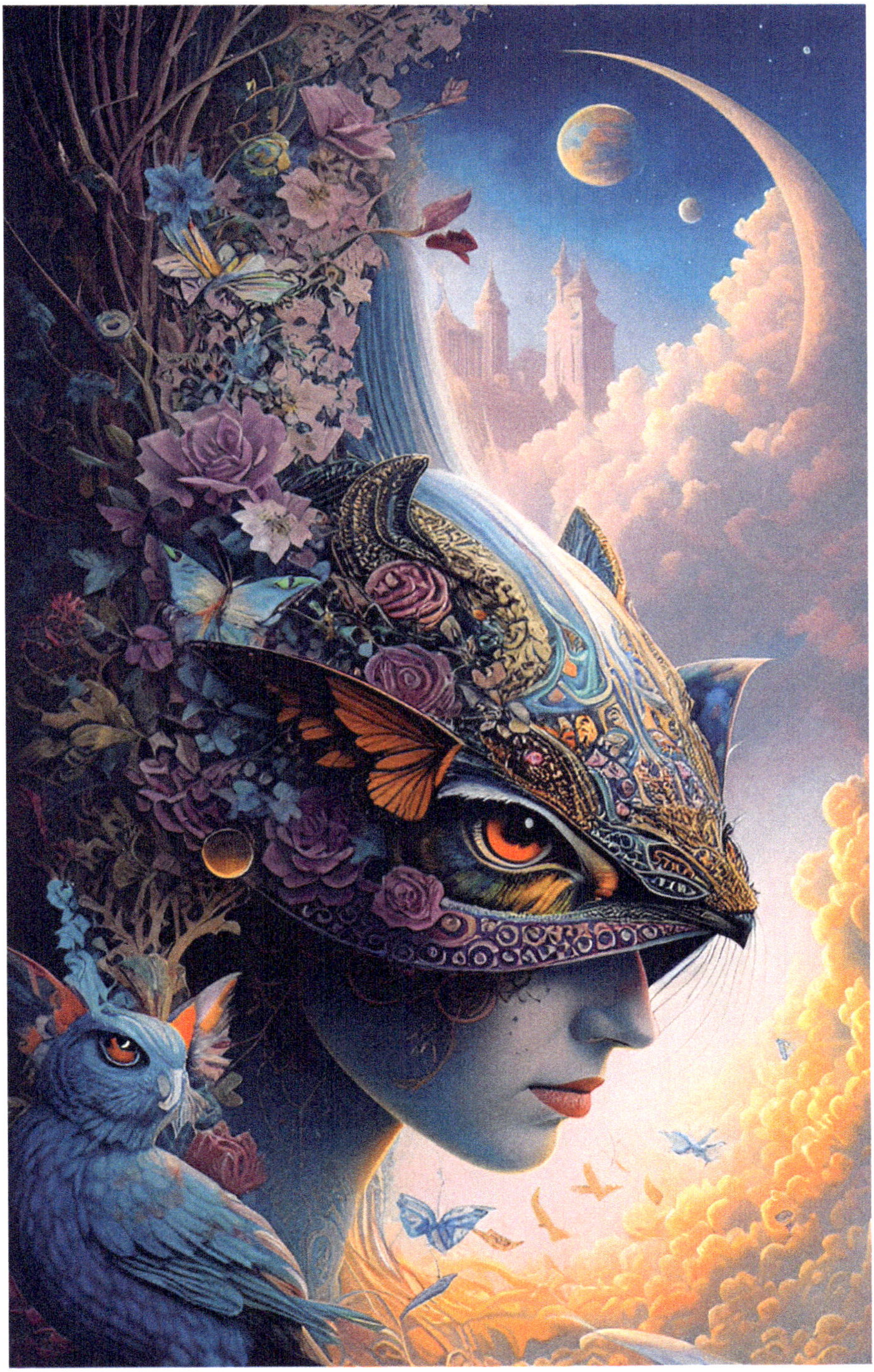

Close your eyes and still the time around you. Can you feel the story coming alive within you? What do you need to alter to create a new experience? Allow yourself to be enveloped by the possibilities unfurling before you. What will you see? What will you feel in the depths of this new story?

Please write it down or stare at this empty page until it is filled with visions of magic, mystery and transformation.

Enjoy yourself!

5 SELF-LOVE AND RADICAL ACCEPTANCE

In the mystical land of Luminara, nestled within the embrace of majestic mountains and lush, verdant valleys, there lived a magical and beautiful witch named Aurora. Aurora was known throughout Luminara for her tireless exploration of the realm's hidden corners and her insatiable thirst for knowledge. However, beneath her adventurous spirit, Aurora harbored a secret – she struggled with insecurity and self-doubt, unable to fully accept herself for who she was.

As the years passed, Aurora's insecurities began to take their toll on her spirit, and she found herself longing for a way to overcome her inner turmoil. Determined to find the answers she sought, Aurora embarked on a journey of self-discovery, venturing far and wide in search of the wisdom that would help her develop compassion for herself and embrace her true nature.

Her journey led her to many extraordinary places, from the highest peaks of the Cloudsong Mountains to the deepest depths of the Crystal Caverns. Along the way, Aurora encountered wise sages and mystical creatures, each offering their unique insights into the nature of self-love and self-acceptance.

One particularly memorable encounter took place in the heart of the Enchanted Forest, where Aurora met a wise, ancient tree named Elowen. Elowen spoke softly to Aurora, sharing her knowledge of self-compassion and the importance of embracing one's true self.

"Dear Aurora," Elowen whispered, "To truly love and accept yourself, you must first learn to let go of the expectations that bind you and embrace the imperfections that make you who you are. You are a beautiful, magical being, and your uniqueness is your greatest strength."

Inspired by Elowen's words, Aurora began to practice self-compassion, learning to treat herself with the same kindness and understanding that she would offer to others. She meditated beneath the boughs of Elowen, allowing her gentle wisdom to permeate her soul and guide her on her path to self-acceptance.

As Aurora continued her journey, she discovered that the key to self-love lay not in striving for perfection, but in recognizing and embracing her own unique qualities and strengths. She learned to celebrate her successes and forgive herself for her shortcomings, understanding that self-acceptance is an ongoing process, one that requires patience and persistence.

With each new day and each new adventure, Aurora's self-love and self-compassion grew stronger, and her insecurities began to fade into the shadows of the past. She found solace in the knowledge that she was not alone in her struggles, that every being in Luminara faced their own battles and sought their own form of self-acceptance.

As Aurora's light shone brighter, her story spread throughout the land, inspiring others to embark on their own journeys of self-discovery and self-love. Through her experiences, Aurora became a beacon of hope and a testament to the transformative power of self-acceptance.

And so, the magical and beautiful witch, once plagued by insecurity and self-doubt, found peace and happiness within herself. By embracing her true nature and learning the importance of self-compassion, Aurora not only transformed her own life but also became a guiding light for those who sought the same path of self-discovery and self-love.

55 WITCHES

Close your eyes and still the time around you. Can you feel the story coming alive within you? What do you need to alter to create a new experience? Allow yourself to be enveloped by the possibilities unfurling before you. What will you see? What will you feel in the depths of this new story?

Please write it down or stare at this empty page until it is filled with visions of magic, mystery and transformation.

Enjoy yourself!

6 LIFE EXPLORER

Once upon a time, a beautiful, clever, and fortunate witch named Ingrid lived. She had a gift unlike any other: she knew the names of all the things and creatures in the world and could bring anything to life with a wave of her wand.

Ingrid's gift attracted all kinds of magical creatures. Talking birds and animals flocked to her, and strange creatures with mysterious gifts appeared before her. No one had ever seen these apparitions before, but they all seemed drawn to Ingrid.

One of her dearest companions was a huge spider that weaved tales as if they were old stories. The spider's tales were so charming that Ingrid could often sit and listen to them for hours.

Ingrid also had a special relationship with the sea mermaids. They sang haunting melodies to her that could heal any heartache. Ingrid collected these songs in glass bottles and gave them to those who needed them.

Ingrid was not afraid to travel in the darkness, where the spirits of antiquity dwelt, coming and going in the blink of an eye. She explored caves filled with clear and transparent gems that seemed to be made of stars and secret gardens where all sorts of magical beings lived peacefully. They all told her their stories.

One day, while exploring the secret garden, Ingrid discovered a hidden path that led her to a magnificent palace. Inside she found a beautiful prince who was trapped by an evil sorceress.

Ingrid realized she had to save the prince. She used her wit and luck to outwit the sorceress, and with a wave of her wand, she broke the spell that trapped the prince.

The prince was grateful to Ingrid and asked her to stay with him in the palace. But Ingrid knew that her place was not in the palace. She had a mission to explore the enchanted lands and work her magic wherever she found herself.

So Ingrid continued her journey, accompanied by all the magical creatures she had befriended. She knew there were many more stories waiting to be told, and she couldn't wait to learn them all.

And so Ingrid, the beautiful, clever, and fortunate witch, continued to work her magic in the enchanted land, bringing joy and amazement to all who crossed her path.

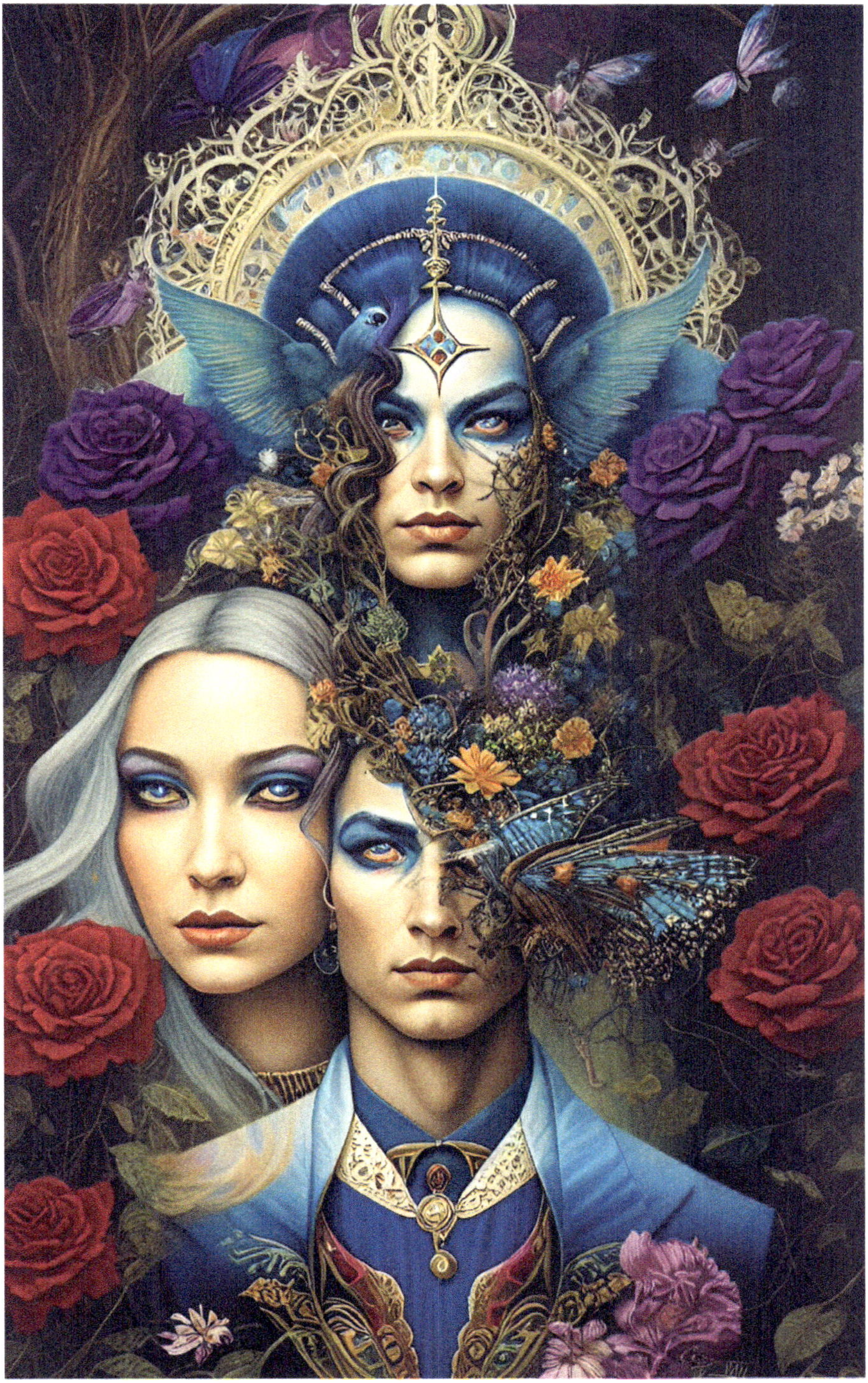

Close your eyes and still the time around you. Can you feel the story coming alive within you? What do you need to alter to create a new experience? Allow yourself to be enveloped by the possibilities unfurling before you. What will you see? What will you feel in the depths of this new story?

Please write it down or stare at this empty page until it is filled with visions of magic, mystery and transformation.

Enjoy yourself!

7 THE SOLO

Once upon a time, there was a beautiful, clever, and lucky witch named Aurora. Aurora was born with a special gift of learning and mastering magic in a way that no one had seen before. She spent her youth traveling the world, collecting knowledge, and discovering the secrets of life.

As Aurora grew older, her magical powers grew stronger, and she eventually gained the gift of immortality. She lived for centuries, watching the world change around her but never changing herself. She had seen everything there was to see and had done everything there was to do. The world had lost its magic, and Aurora had lost her interest in life.

One day, Aurora decided she needed to do something to regain her interest in life. So she traveled deep into the forest, seeking the wisdom of the wise old tree that was said to hold the universe's secrets.

The tree greeted Aurora with a creaking voice, and Aurora asked, "Wise old tree, I have learned all the secrets of life, gained immortality, and yet I am still not satisfied. How can I regain my interest in life?"

The tree replied, "Aurora, you have learned much, but you have forgotten one important thing. Life is not just about knowledge and power but also about love and connection. You have been alive for centuries, but you have never truly lived."

Aurora was taken aback by the tree's words. She had never considered the value of love and connection before. The tree continued, "To truly live, you must connect with the world and the people around you. You must learn to appreciate the beauty in every moment, even the mundane ones. You must open your heart to the possibility of love and be willing to take risks."

Aurora realized that the wise old tree was right. She had been so focused on gaining knowledge and power that she had forgotten the true value of life. She thanked the tree and made a promise to herself to start living.

From that day on, Aurora made a conscious effort to connect with the world around her. She found joy in the simple things, like the warmth of the sun on her skin or the sound of the birds singing in the morning. She started to make connections with the people around her, even falling in love with a mortal man.

With her newfound appreciation for life, Aurora began to see the world in a new light. She realized that the world was full of magic and wonder and that she had only scratched the surface of what was possible. With a renewed sense of purpose, Aurora continued to learn, but this time, she did it with the understanding that the true secret of life was not knowledge but love and connection.

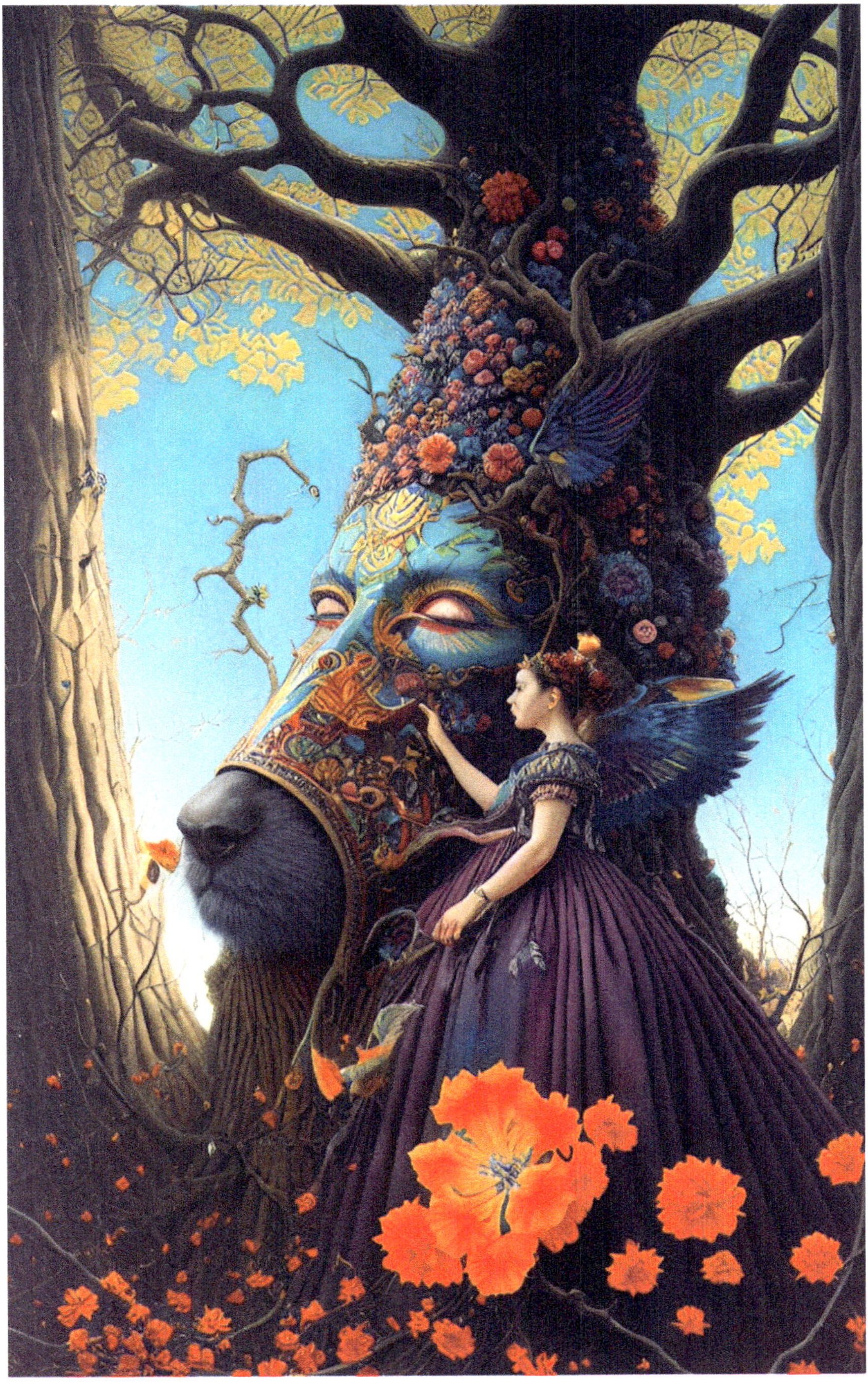

Close your eyes and still the time around you. Can you feel the story coming alive within you? What do you need to alter to create a new experience? Allow yourself to be enveloped by the possibilities unfurling before you. What will you see? What will you feel in the depths of this new story?

Please write it down or stare at this empty page until it is filled with visions of magic, mystery and transformation.

Enjoy yourself!

8 THE SIMPLE THINGS

In a far-off land, there lived a beautiful, smart, and lucky witch named Lyra. She had traveled through time to see and try everything, and in the process, she had learned the ten most important things in the world.

Lyra had seen the beginning of time, the end of time, and everything in between. She had experienced the rise and fall of civilizations, seen wars and peace, and met the most incredible people in history.

But one day, Lyra woke up feeling different. She no longer felt the same sense of wonder and excitement she had always felt before. She had seen and tried everything, and it had all become monotonous.

Lyra decided to embark on the most dangerous and beautiful journey of her life. She would travel to the edge of the universe, to the place where time began, and she would find the meaning of everything.

Lyra knew that this journey would be perilous, but she was determined to see it through. She boarded her time machine, and with a flick of a switch, she was catapulted through time and space.

The journey was long and dangerous. Lyra encountered fierce storms, black holes, and supernovas, but she pressed on. She knew that the answer to the meaning of everything lay at the edge of the universe, and she would not stop until she found it.

After months of traveling, Lyra finally arrived at the edge of the universe. She stepped out of her time machine and looked around. It was the most beautiful thing she had ever seen. The stars were so close she could touch them, and the colors of the galaxy were more vibrant than anything she had ever witnessed.

Lyra realized that she had been searching for the meaning of life in all the wrong places. It wasn't about seeing and trying everything; it was about appreciating the beauty and wonder of the universe.

She had learned the ten most important things in the world, but she had forgotten the most crucial thing of all. To truly live, you had to appreciate the small things, the things that make life worth living.

Lyra returned to her time machine and traveled back to her own time with a renewed sense of purpose. She knew that the true meaning of life was not something to be found at the edge of the universe but something that could be found in the smallest things.

From that day on, Lyra lived her life differently. She appreciated the beauty of every moment, and she no longer searched for the next big adventure. She had found the meaning of everything, and it was in the simplest of things, like the sound of a bird singing, the touch of a loved one, or the smell of freshly baked bread.

Lyra realized that life was a journey, and the destination was not as important as the journey itself. She had traveled to the edge of the universe and back, and in doing so, she had found the true meaning of life.

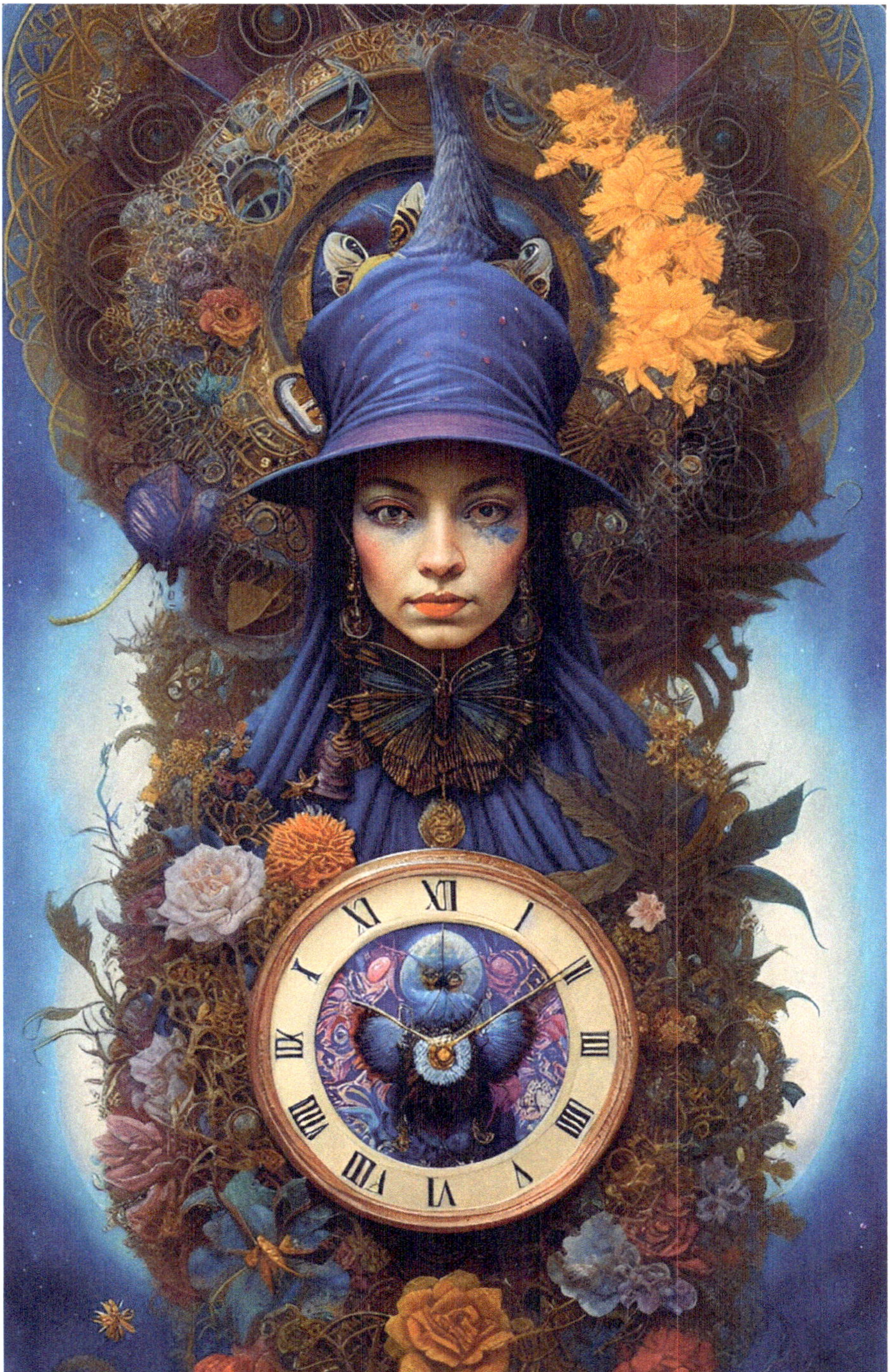
XII
I
II
III
IIII
V
VI
VII
VIII
IX
X
XI

Close your eyes and still the time around you. Can you feel the story coming alive within you? What do you need to alter to create a new experience? Allow yourself to be enveloped by the possibilities unfurling before you. What will you see? What will you feel in the depths of this new story?

Please write it down or stare at this empty page until it is filled with visions of magic, mystery and transformation.

Enjoy yourself!

9 GIVING UP THE GIFT

Once upon a time, there was a witch named Isadora in a kingdom far, far away. She was known throughout the land for her stunning beauty, clever mind, and extraordinary luck. She could cast spells that no one else could, and she used her gift to help others.

One day, Isadora met an ordinary man named Jack. He was kind and loving, and Isadora soon fell deeply in love with him. She hoped for unbelievable happiness, and she was willing to do anything to be with him. So, she made a choice that would change her life forever: she gave up her gift.

At first, Isadora was overjoyed. She spent every moment with Jack, and she loved him more and more each day. But as time went on, she began to feel restless and bored. She missed the thrill of using her gift, and she longed for the power that it had given her.

Isadora realized that love alone was not enough for her. She had given up too much, and she had lost a part of herself in the process. She knew that she needed to find a way to regain her gift, no matter the cost.

So, Isadora set out on a journey to find a way to regain her gift. She traveled far and wide, facing dangers and overcoming obstacles. Eventually, she found a powerful sorcerer who promised to help her.

The sorcerer gave Isadora a potion that would restore her gift but warned her that it would come with a price. Isadora accepted the potion, and the moment she drank it, she felt her powers return.

But as she began to use her gift again, she realized that

something was different. Her love for Jack had faded, and her desire for power had grown. She had lost sight of what was truly important, and she had paid a heavy price for it.

Isadora realized that true happiness could not be found in power or love alone. It came from within, from being true to oneself and living a life of purpose and meaning. She knew that she had a lot to learn, but she was grateful for the lessons that she had learned along the way.

And so, Isadora set out on a new journey, determined to use her gift to help others once again, but this time with a new perspective on life and a new appreciation for the simple things. She had learned that happiness was not about what one had but about how one lived their life, and she was ready to live hers to the fullest.

55 WITCHES

Close your eyes and still the time around you. Can you feel the story coming alive within you? What do you need to alter to create a new experience? Allow yourself to be enveloped by the possibilities unfurling before you. What will you see? What will you feel in the depths of this new story?

Please write it down or stare at this empty page until it is filled with visions of magic, mystery and transformation.

Enjoy yourself!

10 THE LOST HEART

Once upon a time, in a land far away, there was a beautiful witch named Seraphina. She was known throughout the kingdom for her intelligence, her good fortune, and her stunning beauty. People came from all over to seek her advice, and she never failed to impress them with her wit and her charm.

But one day, Seraphina woke up feeling strange. She looked in the mirror and realized that her heart was missing. She had no idea where it had gone or how she had lost it, but she knew that she had to find it. She searched high and low, asking everyone she met if they had seen it, but no one could help her.

Desperate to find her heart, Seraphina decided to go underground. She entered the dark labyrinths of sadness and wandered for days, losing track of time and hope. She was lost and alone, and she didn't know if she would ever find her heart.

Finally, Seraphina emerged from the underground and rose above the clouds, hoping that the white, thick fog would bring her some clarity. She wandered in the mist for what felt like an eternity, but still, she found no trace of her heart.

Just when she was about to give up, Seraphina heard a whisper in the wind. It was a voice that she recognized as her own, but it was speaking words that she had never heard before. "Your heart is not something to be found, Seraphina," the voice said. "It is something to be given away."

Seraphina was struck by the wisdom of the words. She realized that she had been looking for her heart in all the wrong places. She had been searching for something that she had always possessed within herself. She closed her eyes, took a deep breath, and felt her heart return to her chest.

From that day on, Seraphina understood that the true power of love is not in possessing it but in sharing it with others. So she continued using her intelligence and good fortune to help those in need, and she remained one of the most beautiful witches in the land, both inside and out. And whenever she encountered someone who was lost, she would share her story and offer them a glimmer of hope that they, too, could find their heart.

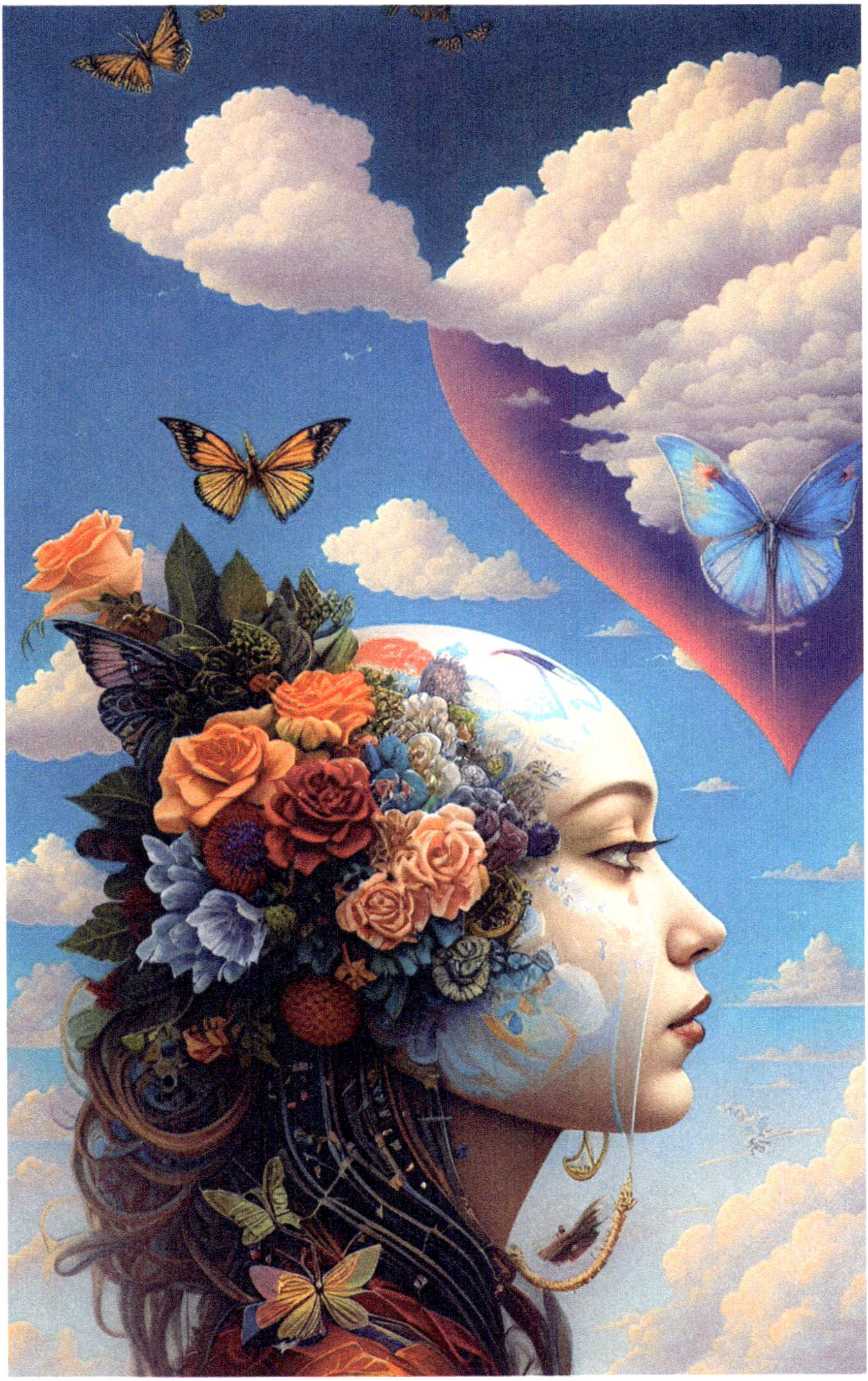

Close your eyes and still the time around you. Can you feel the story coming alive within you? What do you need to alter to create a new experience? Allow yourself to be enveloped by the possibilities unfurling before you. What will you see? What will you feel in the depths of this new story?

Please write it down or stare at this empty page until it is filled with visions of magic, mystery and transformation.

Enjoy yourself!

11 FEARFUL

There once was a witch named Emma who was afraid of everything. Every day, she would wake up with a sense of dread, fearing an instant death, a terrible illness, failure in business, or unhappy love. She was afraid of getting very fat and then getting very thin. She was afraid of losing something, afraid of missing something. And so her life went on in a constant state of fear and anxiety.

Emma had a good job, a loving family, and many friends, but she couldn't shake the feeling that something terrible was always about to happen. She spent her days worrying about the future and regretting the past. She was so consumed by fear that she had stopped enjoying the present moment.

One day, Emma was walking through the park when she saw an old man sitting on a bench. He had a kind face and a twinkle in his eye, and Emma felt drawn to him. So she approached him and asked if she could sit down and talk. The old man welcomed her, and they began to chat.

As they talked, Emma realized that the old man was wise beyond his years. He listened to her fears and concerns and offered her words of comfort and advice. He told her that fear was natural, but it could also be paralyzing. He said that the key to overcoming fear was to face it head-on.

At first, Emma was skeptical. She had tried to overcome her fears many times before, but they always seemed to come back. But the old man was persistent, and he gently encouraged her to take small steps toward facing her fears.

Emma started small. She would take a different route to work or try a new type of food. She would talk to strangers or do something spontaneous. Each time she faced a fear, she felt a little bit braver.

As the days went on, Emma began to feel a sense of liberation. She was no longer held captive by her fears. She was free to enjoy the world around her and to live life to the fullest. She tried new things, met new people, and found joy in the small moments.

But then, one day, Emma faced her biggest fear. She was offered a promotion at work that would require her to move to a new city. The thought of leaving everything she knew and loved was terrifying. But she remembered the old man's words, and she decided to take a leap of faith.

Emma moved to the new city, and at first, it was tough. She missed her family and her friends, and she struggled to adjust to her new surroundings. But she persevered, and before she knew it, she had built a new life for herself. She made new friends, explored new places, and found success in her job.

Emma realized that by facing her fear head-on, she had opened up a world of opportunities. She was no longer held back by her anxieties. She was free to live the life she had always wanted.

As the years went by, Emma never forgot the wise old man who had helped her overcome her fears. She would often think of him and the lessons he had taught her. And whenever she felt a tinge of fear or anxiety creeping in, she would take a deep breath and remember that she was strong and capable.

Emma learned that life is full of uncertainties and that fear is a natural part of the human experience. But she also learned that fear should never hold one back from living life to the fullest. She was grateful for the lessons she had learned and was happy to live a life free from fear.

55 WITCHES

Close your eyes and still the time around you. Can you feel the story coming alive within you? What do you need to alter to create a new experience? Allow yourself to be enveloped by the possibilities unfurling before you. What will you see? What will you feel in the depths of this new story?

Please write it down or stare at this empty page until it is filled with visions of magic, mystery and transformation.

Enjoy yourself!

12 THE SKEPTICAL

In a land far away, there lived a beautiful, clever, and lucky witch named Aurora. She had been blessed with powerful magic from birth, but her skepticism often got in the way of her using her powers to their full potential.

Aurora had always been skeptical of her abilities, constantly questioning whether her magic was real or just a figment of her imagination. As a result, she often held back from using her powers, afraid of what might happen if they didn't work.

One day, Aurora decided that she had had enough of her skepticism holding her back. She set out on a quest to prove herself wrong and to unlock her true potential.

As Aurora traveled through the enchanted forest, she met a group of animals who would become her new friends. There was a wise old owl, a cunning fox, and a loyal wolf, and they all decided to join her on her quest.

The group soon came across a village that was in great peril. A wicked sorcerer had cursed the village, the crops were dying, and the people were becoming ill. Aurora knew that this was her chance to prove herself wrong and to help those in need.

She gathered her newfound friends and set out to break the curse. They encountered many challenges along the way, but Aurora refused to give up. She started to believe in herself and her abilities, and with each success, her powers grew stronger.

As they arrived at the sorcerer's castle, Aurora's powers were at their peak. She believed in herself, and her skepticism had vanished, replaced with a newfound confidence in her magic.

With the help of her friends, Aurora broke the curse and saved the village. The people cheered, and Aurora felt a sense of accomplishment she had never experienced before.

From that day on, Aurora continued to use her powers to help those in need. She no longer held back from using her magic, and her newfound confidence had unlocked her true potential.

Aurora had learned an important lesson on her quest. She had learned that the only thing holding her back from achieving greatness was her own skepticism. By believing in herself, she unlocked her true potential and became the most powerful witch in all the land.

Close your eyes and still the time around you. Can you feel the story coming alive within you? What do you need to alter to create a new experience? Allow yourself to be enveloped by the possibilities unfurling before you. What will you see? What will you feel in the depths of this new story?

Please write it down or stare at this empty page until it is filled with visions of magic, mystery and transformation.

Enjoy yourself!

13 TRAVELER TO LOST CITIES

Traveler to Lost Cities. In a land where magic was the norm, there lived a powerful witch named Lyra. She had heard stories of a lost city hidden deep within the enchanted lands, filled with magical treasures and secrets waiting to be uncovered. Lyra had always been fascinated with the unknown, so she decided to set out on a dangerous journey to discover this lost city and uncover its secrets.

As Lyra traveled through the enchanted lands, she encountered wonders beyond her wildest dreams. Trees that talked and granted wishes, rivers that glowed with the light of a thousand stars, and fish that held conversations with each other. She explored dark caves, swam in shimmering ponds filled with chattering fish, and flew on the backs of giant eagles to discover secret kingdoms hidden high up in ice-capped mountaintops.

Along the way, Lyra met allies and enemies alike who tested her courage and magical abilities. She encountered mischievous fairies who played tricks on her, fierce dragons who guarded hidden treasures, and unicorns who only revealed themselves to those with pure hearts.

But Lyra was not easily deterred. She used her cleverness and luck to overcome the obstacles in her path and her magic to defeat those who stood in her way. She even discovered ancient spells that had been lost for centuries, unlocking new levels of power within herself.

As she neared the lost city, Lyra faced her greatest challenge yet. A powerful sorcerer had laid a trap for her, using dark magic to try and stop her from uncovering the secrets of the lost city.

But Lyra was not afraid. She summoned all of her power and defeated the sorcerer, breaking the spell and uncovering the lost city.

Inside, she found wonders beyond her wildest dreams. Ancient artifacts, magical treasures, and secrets that had been lost for centuries. Lyra knew that she had unlocked something truly special, and her journey had been worth every moment.

As she returned home, Lyra knew that her journey had changed her. She had become wiser, stronger, and more confident in her abilities. And she knew many more journeys and mysteries were waiting to be uncovered in the enchanted lands.

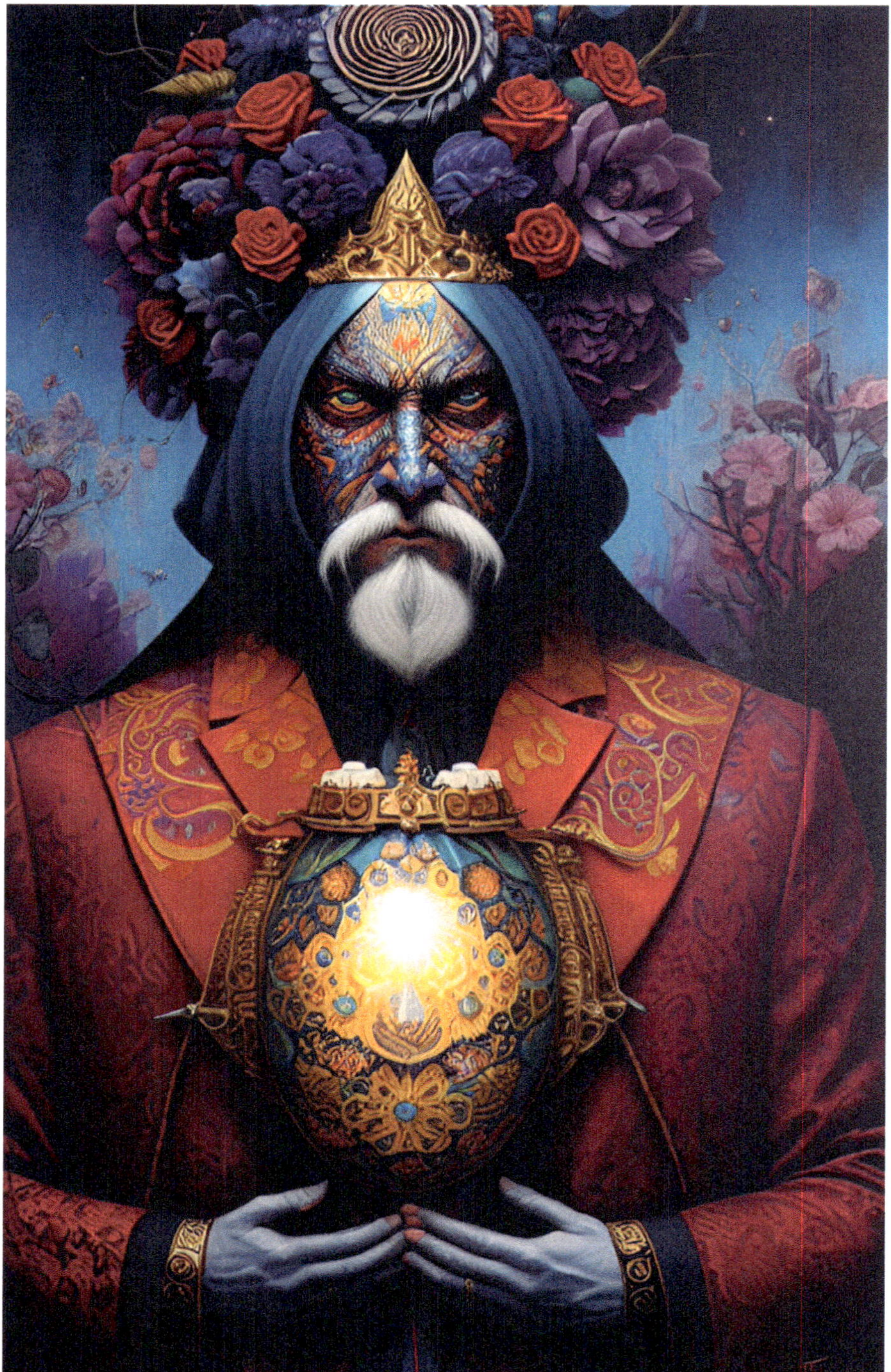

Close your eyes and still the time around you. Can you feel the story coming alive within you? What do you need to alter to create a new experience? Allow yourself to be enveloped by the possibilities unfurling before you. What will you see? What will you feel in the depths of this new story?

Please write it down or stare at this empty page until it is filled with visions of magic, mystery and transformation.

Enjoy yourself!

14 SELF-HEALING

In a far-off land lived a beautiful, clever, and lucky witch named Celeste. She had lived for centuries and learned all the secrets of life. She had been blessed with immortality and could understand all people of the world.

One day, Celeste fell ill. She had never been sick before, and it was a new experience for her. She tried all the spells and potions she knew, but nothing seemed to work. Finally, she knew that she needed a rare herb that could only be found in a dark forest far away.

Celeste set out on her journey, determined to find the herb and cure her illness. As she entered the dark forest, she saw that it was filled with dangers. Poisonous plants, dangerous animals, and treacherous terrain lay in her path.

But Celeste was clever and lucky. She had learned to navigate through dangerous situations with her wit and cunning. She used her magic to create a protective shield around herself and moved carefully through the forest.

As she searched for the rare herb, Celeste encountered a variety of creatures. Some were friendly and helpful, while others were unfriendly and posed a threat. She used her ability to understand all people to communicate with them and overcome the obstacles in her path.

Finally, after many trials and tribulations, Celeste found the rare herb that she needed. She prepared a potion with the herb, and it worked. Her illness vanished, and she felt renewed.

On her journey back, Celeste realized that she had learned a valuable lesson. She had always thought that her immortality would keep her safe from harm, but she now knew that even the most powerful witches could become ill or face danger.

She realized that no one was invincible and that sometimes the only way to overcome a challenge was to face it head-on with determination, wit, and courage.

As Celeste returned home, she knew that her journey had changed her. She had learned to appreciate the fragility of life and to value the importance of taking risks. She knew that there were still many secrets to uncover, and she was ready to face them with newfound strength and wisdom.

Close your eyes and still the time around you. Can you feel the story coming alive within you? What do you need to alter to create a new experience? Allow yourself to be enveloped by the possibilities unfurling before you. What will you see? What will you feel in the depths of this new story?

Please write it down or stare at this empty page until it is filled with visions of magic, mystery and transformation.

Enjoy yourself!

15 COPING WITH THE SHADOWS

In a magical land, a beautiful, clever, and lucky witch named Isadora lived. She had everything she ever wanted - power, wealth, and love. Unfortunately, she had fallen in love with a man named Liam, who was kind and charming. They had planned to spend their lives together, but one day, Liam was suddenly taken away by the shadows.

Isadora knew that she had to do everything in her power to save Liam. She learned of a way to travel to the realm of shadows, where she could find and rescue him.

Isadora set out on her journey, using her magic to travel through different dimensions until she arrived in the realm of shadows. But as soon as she arrived, something strange happened. She forgot everything - who she was and why she had come here.

Isadora soon realized that the realm of shadows held many dangers. The shadows were creatures of the night, and they were not friendly to outsiders. They had their own rules, and anyone who broke them would be punished severely.

Isadora was lost and alone in this strange world. She wandered through the shadows, trying to find Liam. She encountered many dangers along the way - creatures with sharp teeth, traps that would ensnare her, and illusions that would confuse her.

But Isadora was lucky, and she managed to overcome each challenge. She had a clever mind, and she used her wit and magic to outsmart the creatures of the night.

As she traveled deeper into the realm of shadows, Isadora started to remember who she was and why she had come here. She remembered Liam and her love for him, and she knew that she had to find him.

Finally, after many trials and tribulations, Isadora found Liam. But he was not the same as before. The shadows had changed him, and he was no longer the kind and charming man that Isadora had fallen in love with.

Isadora knew that she had to do everything in her power to save Liam. She used her magic to fight against the shadows and to break the curse that had been put on him.

In the end, Isadora was successful, and Liam was restored to his former self. They returned to their world, grateful for the love and luck that had brought them back together.

Isadora had learned an important lesson on her journey - that the realm of shadows held many dangers, but with her cleverness and luck, she was able to overcome them all. And even when she had forgotten everything, her love for Liam had remained strong, guiding her through the darkness.

Close your eyes and still the time around you. Can you feel the story coming alive within you? What do you need to alter to create a new experience? Allow yourself to be enveloped by the possibilities unfurling before you. What will you see? What will you feel in the depths of this new story?

Please write it down or stare at this empty page until it is filled with visions of magic, mystery and transformation.

Enjoy yourself!

16 WEAVING DREAMS

There was a beautiful, clever, and dreamy witch named Isabella who could weave dreams. She read people's thoughts and chose the most beautiful and clear ones. She would catch the tip of a thought, wind it on her thin finger, and then spin it into magical canvases of dreams. The dreams were very different, and the people who dreamed them sometimes wondered how they could have been dreamed.

One day as Isabella was weaving dreams, she came across a thought that was unlike any she had ever seen before. It was the thought of a young woman who dreamed of becoming a witch like Isabella.

Isabella was intrigued by this thought, and she decided to weave a dream for this girl. She wove the dream into a magical cloth and sent it to the woman.

The woman, whose name was Lila, was struck by the dream. It was so vivid and real that she felt herself becoming a witch. She was so grateful to Isabella that she decided to seek her out.

Lila set out on a journey to find Isabella. She traveled through enchanted forests and swam across crystal-clear rivers until she finally reached Isabella's home.

When she arrived, Isabella welcomed her with open arms. She saw potential in Lila and realized that she could help her become a witch. She took Lila under her wing and taught her everything she knew about magic.

Lila learned quickly and absorbed everything Isabella taught her. She learned to read people's minds, weave dreams, and cast powerful spells. She became as beautiful and clever and dreamy as Isabella.

Together, Isabella and Lila wove dreams for people all over the land. They created magical canvases that transported people to different worlds and showed them things they had never seen before. They became famous for their dream weaving, and people came from all over the world to have these two witches weave their dreams.

But even with all their success, Isabella knew she was missing something. She had always dreamed of going to the ends of the earth and exploring the unknown. She'd been so busy dream-weaving that she'd never had the chance to do it.

So Isabella and Lila set out on a journey to explore the unknown. They traveled through enchanted lands, crossed boundless oceans, and climbed towering mountains. They encountered many dangers along the way, but they used their magic and wit to overcome them.

As they traveled, Isabella realized that she had found something she had been missing. The journey made her see life in a new way, and she felt more alive than ever before.

In the end, Isabella and Lila returned home wiser and stronger than ever before. They continued to weave dreams for people all over the land, but now they did so with a newfound sense of purpose and adventure. And every time they weaved a dream, they remembered their incredible journey and the magic that had brought them together.

MONETA AGENCY

Close your eyes and still the time around you. Can you feel the story coming alive within you? What do you need to alter to create a new experience? Allow yourself to be enveloped by the possibilities unfurling before you. What will you see? What will you feel in the depths of this new story?

Please write it down or stare at this empty page until it is filled with visions of magic, mystery and transformation.

Enjoy yourself!

17 THE RESCUE

Once upon a time, a beautiful, clever, and lucky witch named Selena lived in a magical land. She had learned all the secrets of life, gained immortality, and lived for centuries. But one day, Selena woke up feeling restless and uninterested in everything.

She decided to take a break from her usual routine and took a stroll through the enchanted forest. There, she met an immortal being named Orion, who was as old as time itself. They quickly fell in love, and the handsome and charming Orion swept Selena off her feet.

However, Selena soon learned that immortality came with a cost. She saw that Orion had experienced so much loss and pain throughout his long life. He had seen countless civilizations rise and fall, and he had outlived so many loved ones.

Selena realized that even though immortality could be a gift, it was also a curse. She saw that the weight of immortality had taken its toll on Orion, and he was tired of living.

Selena knew that she had to do something to help her love regain his zest for life. She set out on a journey to find a way to lift the burden of immortality from Orion's shoulders.

She traveled to the ends of the earth, learning from powerful witches and wizards, and consulted with the most knowledgeable beings. She finally found an ancient and powerful potion that could grant temporary mortality to the immortals.

Selena took the potion back to Orion, and he eagerly drank it. The potion transformed him into a mortal being, and he was able to experience life as he had never done before. He felt the wind on his face, the sun on his skin, and the warmth of love in his heart.

Together, Selena and Orion lived a full life, experiencing everything life had to offer, from the smallest joys to the most significant challenges. They traveled the world, met incredible people, and experienced true love.

As time passed, Orion's mortality started to wear off, and Selena knew that she had to make a decision. She could either leave Orion behind, knowing that he would be immortal again, or she could give up her own immortality to be with him.

Selena decided to give up her immortality and live a mortal life with Orion. She knew that life was fleeting and that true love was worth any sacrifice.

Selena and Orion lived the rest of their lives together, and even when they passed away, their love story lived on as an inspiration to all who heard it.

Close your eyes and still the time around you. Can you feel the story coming alive within you? What do you need to alter to create a new experience? Allow yourself to be enveloped by the possibilities unfurling before you. What will you see? What will you feel in the depths of this new story?

Please write it down or stare at this empty page until it is filled with visions of magic, mystery and transformation.

Enjoy yourself!

18 KNOWING THE FUTURE

Zoey was a beautiful, clever, and lucky witch who had a special gift - she could see the future of anyone she met. When she looked at a person, she saw their fate and the path that lay ahead of them. But she never told anyone what she saw for fear of spoiling their future.

Zoey lived a quiet life, using her gift to help people in small ways. She would use her magic to nudge them in the right direction, to help them avoid the pitfalls that lay ahead.

One day, Zoey met a man named Ethan. He was kind and charming, and she felt drawn to him. But when she looked into his future, she saw that he was destined for great hardship and pain.

Zoey knew that she had a choice to make. She could either tell Ethan what she saw and risk spoiling his future, or she could keep it to herself and let him follow his path.

After much contemplation, Zoey decided not to tell Ethan. She knew that the future was not set in stone and that he could still find happiness despite the challenges that lay ahead.

As Zoey and Ethan grew closer, Zoey watched as he faced one trial after another. Each time, she used her magic to help him, guiding him through the obstacles that lay in his path.

Over time, Ethan began to notice that Zoey always seemed to know what was coming next. He asked her how she did it, and she told him about her gift. Ethan was amazed, and he asked her why she had never told him before.

Zoey explained that she did not want to spoil his future and that she believed that he could still find happiness despite the challenges that lay ahead.

Ethan was grateful to Zoey, and he knew that he had found someone special. He asked her to be his partner in life, and Zoey accepted.

Together, they faced the challenges that lay ahead, but with Zoey's guidance and Ethan's determination, they were able to overcome them all. They found happiness and love, and they knew that their future was bright.

Zoey had learned an important lesson - that the future was not set in stone and that even the hardest challenges could be overcome with determination and a little bit of magic. She knew that her gift was a blessing, and she would continue to use it to help others in small ways, knowing that even the smallest actions could make a big difference.

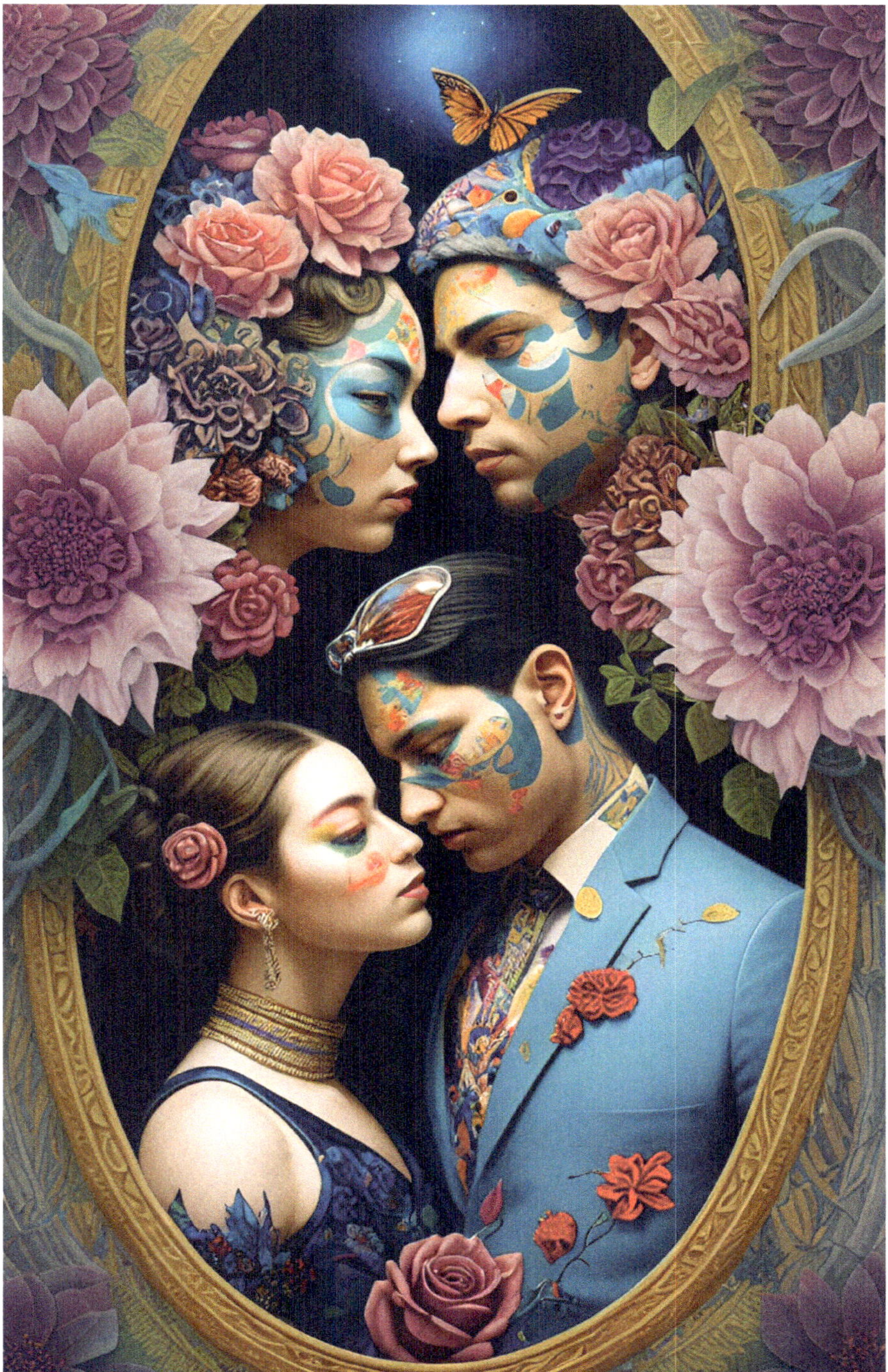

Close your eyes and still the time around you. Can you feel the story coming alive within you? What do you need to alter to create a new experience? Allow yourself to be enveloped by the possibilities unfurling before you. What will you see? What will you feel in the depths of this new story?

Please write it down or stare at this empty page until it is filled with visions of magic, mystery and transformation.

Enjoy yourself!

19 WALKING THROUGH THE WALLS

Rosa was a beautiful, clever, and lucky witch who had a unique gift - she could walk through walls. She had always been fascinated by the idea of being able to pass through solid objects, and as she grew older, she discovered that she had the power to do just that.

Rosa used her gift in many ways. She could enter locked rooms or buildings without needing a key. She could sneak past guards and patrols undetected, and she could move quickly and silently through any obstacle in her path.

One day, Rosa was hired to steal a valuable artifact from a wealthy merchant's house. The artifact was locked away in a room that was heavily guarded, and no one had been able to get in.

Rosa knew that this was the perfect job for her. She put on her cloak of invisibility and made her way to the merchant's house. She slipped through the front door and easily made her way past the guards. She then walked through the walls until she found the room where the artifact was stored.

As she made her way through the wall, she suddenly heard a voice. It was the voice of the merchant's daughter, who was locked away in the room. She had been accused of a crime she did not commit and was being held, prisoner.

Rosa was torn. She knew that she had been hired to steal the artifact, but she also knew that she could not leave the young woman locked away in the room. She decided to help the girl and walked through the wall to her side.

With her cleverness and luck, Rosa was able to convince the

guards to release the girl. She then used her powers to retrieve the artifact and return it to the rightful owner, earning a handsome reward.

Rosa had learned an important lesson - that her gift was not just for personal gain. She could use it to help others and make the world a better place. From that day on, she used her gift for good, helping those in need and making a difference in the world.

And although she could still walk through walls, Rosa knew that the greatest power she had was the power to help others and make a positive impact on the world.

Close your eyes and still the time around you. Can you feel the story coming alive within you? What do you need to alter to create a new experience? Allow yourself to be enveloped by the possibilities unfurling before you. What will you see? What will you feel in the depths of this new story?

Please write it down or stare at this empty page until it is filled with visions of magic, mystery and transformation.

Enjoy yourself!

20 THE GIFT OF FLIGHT

Solidate was a beautiful, clever, and lucky witch with the gift of flight. She could soar through the air on a broomstick, her hair whipping in the wind as she traveled to far-off lands.

Solidate loved to explore the world around her, and her gift of flight allowed her to see things from a new perspective. She would travel to the highest peaks of the mountains, where she could see for miles in every direction. She would fly over vast oceans, watching as the waves crashed against the shore below. She would glide through dense forests, marveling at the beauty of the trees and the animals that lived there.

One day, Solidate was flying over a small village when she saw a young girl being chased by a pack of wolves. Solidate knew that she had to help, so she flew down to the ground and used her cleverness and luck to outwit the wolves and save the girl.

The girl was grateful to Solidate, and she asked her to stay and help the village. Solidate agreed, and she used her gift of flight to keep the village safe from harm. She would fly high above the village, keeping a watchful eye on the people below.

Solidate soon became known as the village's protector. The people knew that they could always count on her to keep them safe from harm. She used her cleverness and luck to outwit any dangers that came their way, and her gift of flight allowed her to quickly respond to any emergency.

Over time, Solidate grew to love the village and the people who lived there. She knew that her gift of flight had given her the ability to make a difference in the world, and she was determined to use it for good.

Solidate's adventures continued, but she always made sure to use her gift of flight to help those in need. And although she was a powerful and clever witch, she knew that her greatest strength was her willingness to use her gifts to help others.

Close your eyes and still the time around you. Can you feel the story coming alive within you? What do you need to alter to create a new experience? Allow yourself to be enveloped by the possibilities unfurling before you. What will you see? What will you feel in the depths of this new story?

Please write it down or stare at this empty page until it is filled with visions of magic, mystery and transformation.

Enjoy yourself!

21 THE MAGIC VOICE

Sarah was a beautiful, clever, and lucky witch who had an incredible gift - her singing voice was so enchanting that she could charm anyone who heard her. With just a few notes, she could make even the grumpiest person smile, and her voice was so beautiful that it could bring tears to your eyes.

One day, Sarah found herself in a difficult situation. She had been accused of a crime she did not commit, and she knew that she needed to find a way to clear her name. She decided to use her gift of singing to help her.

Sarah traveled to the palace of the king, knowing that he was a powerful man who could help her. When she arrived, she sang a beautiful song that touched the king's heart. He was so moved by her voice that he offered to help her in any way he could.

Sarah used her cleverness and luck to convince the king that she was innocent. She told him her story, and he was so impressed by her that he decided to clear her name.

Word of Sarah's gift of singing soon spread throughout the kingdom, and people began to seek her out. They would come from far and wide to hear her sing, and they would offer her gifts of all kinds.

Sarah used her gift for good, singing at weddings and other joyous occasions. She would also sing for the sick and the dying, bringing comfort and peace to those who were suffering.

Over time, Sarah became known as the "Singing Witch," and she was loved by all who knew her. Her gift of singing had brought joy and happiness to so many, and she knew that she had made a difference in the world.

And although she could use her gift to get anything she wanted,

Sarah knew that the true power of her gift was in using it to help others. So she continued to sing, bringing happiness and joy to all who heard her, and she knew that her voice would always be her greatest gift.

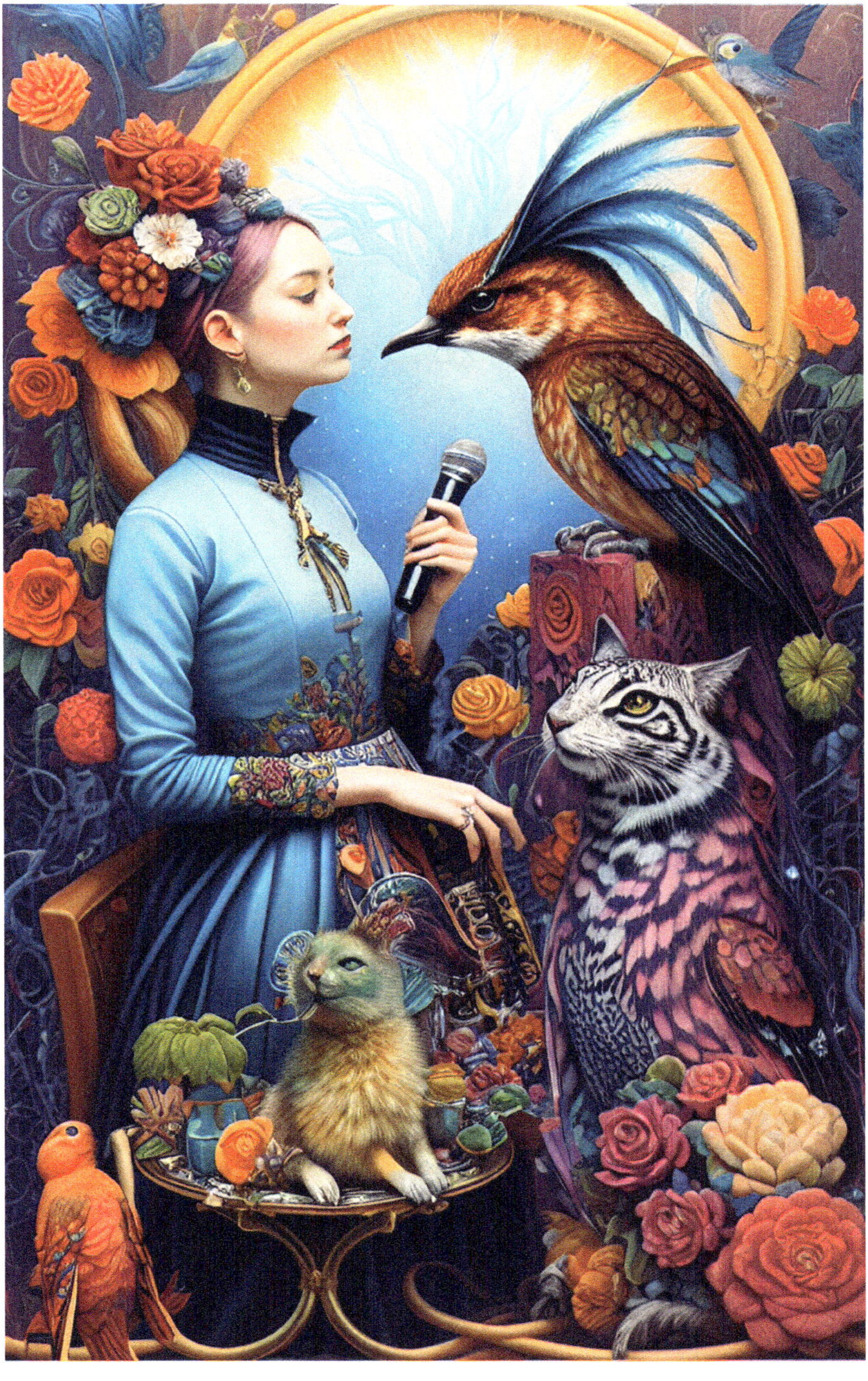

Close your eyes and still the time around you. Can you feel the story coming alive within you? What do you need to alter to create a new experience? Allow yourself to be enveloped by the possibilities unfurling before you. What will you see? What will you feel in the depths of this new story?

Please write it down or stare at this empty page until it is filled with visions of magic, mystery and transformation.

Enjoy yourself!

22 JUST THE WAY I WANT IT

Monica was a beautiful, clever, and bossy witch. She loved to be in control, and she had a gift for creating worlds where everything and everyone obeyed her every command. She had built a magical castle where she lived with her subjects, and she spent her days making sure that everything was just the way she wanted it.

Monica was a perfectionist and had a sharp eye for detail. She wanted everything to be just right, from the way the flowers were arranged in the garden to the way the silverware was placed on the table.

Monica's subjects were all under her spell, and they would do anything to please her. They would work tirelessly to make sure that everything was perfect, and they would never dare to question her authority.

Monica was happy with her world, but deep down, she knew that something was missing. She longed for something more, something that would bring meaning to her life beyond just controlling everything.

One day, a visitor came to Monica's castle. It was a young girl who had lost her way in the woods. Monica welcomed her, but she soon realized that the girl was not under her spell. The girl was free and independent, and she challenged Monica's way of life.

At first, Monica was annoyed by the girl's presence. She tried to control her, just like she did with everyone else. But the girl was different. She refused to be controlled and challenged Monica's way of thinking.

Over time, Monica grew to respect the girl. She realized that there was more to life than just controlling everything. She learned that true happiness came from living a life of freedom, creativity, and independence.

Monica's world changed. She began to see the beauty in imperfection, and she started to let go of her need for control. She still had her subjects, but she no longer controlled every aspect of their lives.

Monica's transformation was not easy, but it was worth it. She learned that true happiness came from letting go of control and embracing the beauty of life. And even though she would always be a bossy witch at heart, she now knew that there was more to life than just being in control.

Close your eyes and still the time around you. Can you feel the story coming alive within you? What do you need to alter to create a new experience? Allow yourself to be enveloped by the possibilities unfurling before you. What will you see? What will you feel in the depths of this new story?

Please write it down or stare at this empty page until it is filled with visions of magic, mystery and transformation.

Enjoy yourself!

23 ALWAYS A WINNER

Lisa was a beautiful, clever, and funny witch. She had a gift for winning at all the games, and she was good at everything she tried. From chess to charades, from card games to sports, Lisa always came out on top.

She loved the thrill of competition and the rush of adrenaline that came with winning. But as time went on, Lisa started to feel like something was missing. She had become so focused on winning that she had forgotten how to have fun.

One day, Lisa decided to take a break from all the games and competitions. She went for a walk in the woods, enjoying the beauty of nature and the peacefulness of being alone. As she walked, she thought about all the times she had won and how it had made her feel.

But as she thought more about it, she realized that winning wasn't everything. She missed the laughter and the joy of playing with others, even if she didn't always win.

Lisa decided to invite some friends over for a game night, but this time, she was determined to have fun and not worry about winning. They played silly games and told funny stories, and Lisa laughed until her sides hurt.

For the first time in a long time, Lisa felt truly happy. She realized that it wasn't about winning or being the best. It was about having fun and enjoying the company of others.

From that day on, Lisa still loved to compete and win, but she never forgot the importance of having fun and enjoying the moment. She learned that sometimes, it's not about winning. It's about the journey and the memories that are made along the way. And even if she didn't always come out on top, she knew that she could still have a good time and make some great memories.

MONETA AGENCY

Close your eyes and still the time around you. Can you feel the story coming alive within you? What do you need to alter to create a new experience? Allow yourself to be enveloped by the possibilities unfurling before you. What will you see? What will you feel in the depths of this new story?

Please write it down or stare at this empty page until it is filled with visions of magic, mystery and transformation.

Enjoy yourself!

24 THE CURIOUS

Stella was a beautiful, intelligent, and funny witch who loved to wander into other people's dreams. She had the ability to enter people's subconscious minds while they slept, and she enjoyed exploring their innermost thoughts and desires.

Stella was a bit of a mischief-maker, and she loved to play pranks on people while they slept. She would create elaborate dream worlds and scenarios, often involving wild adventures and strange characters.

One day, Stella wandered into the dream of a young man named Jack. Jack was having a nightmare, and he was tossing and turning in his sleep. Stella felt a pang of empathy for him and decided to try and help.

She entered his dream and found him trapped in a dark and scary forest. Stella knew that she had to help him escape, but it wouldn't be easy. She conjured up a pair of wings and flew him to safety, dodging monsters and obstacles along the way.

When Jack woke up the next morning, he felt better than he had in weeks. He knew that he had been saved by a mysterious presence in his dream, and he was determined to find out who it was.

Jack eventually discovered Stella and thanked her for saving him. He was amazed by her ability to enter people's dreams and wanted to learn more about her and her powers.

Over time, Stella and Jack became good friends. Stella would visit Jack's dreams often, but she no longer played pranks on him. Instead, she helped him work through his fears and anxieties, giving him the courage he needed to face his challenges in the waking world.

Stella's ability to enter people's dreams has given her the power to make a real difference in people's lives. She realized that her gift was not just about having fun or playing pranks but about helping people overcome their fears and find the courage to face their challenges.

Stella continued exploring people's dreams, but she did so with a new purpose. She knew she had a gift and was determined to use it to make the world a better place.

Close your eyes and still the time around you. Can you feel the story coming alive within you? What do you need to alter to create a new experience? Allow yourself to be enveloped by the possibilities unfurling before you. What will you see? What will you feel in the depths of this new story?

Please write it down or stare at this empty page until it is filled with visions of magic, mystery and transformation.

Enjoy yourself!

25 PARTY GIRL

Calypso was a beautiful, clever, and cheerful witch who loved to have fun like no one else. She was always the life of the party, and everyone loved being around her. Calypso knew how to make people laugh, and her energy was contagious.

One day, Calypso met a man named Alexander. Alexander was different from anyone Calypso had ever met before. He was quiet and reserved and didn't seem to need the same kind of fun and excitement that Calypso did.

At first, Calypso was intrigued by Alexander's calm and collected demeanor. She had never met anyone like him before, and she was curious to know more.

As she got to know Alexander, Calypso realized that he didn't need to have fun in the same way she did. Instead, he was content with just being with her, talking and enjoying each other's company.

Calypso was amazed by Alexander's inner strength and his ability to find joy in the simple things. She realized that she had been so focused on having fun and being the center of attention that she had forgotten to appreciate the beauty in the quiet moments of life.

Over time, Calypso learned to appreciate the simple joys of life. She still loved to have fun and be the life of the party, but she now knew that there was more to life than just that.

She and Alexander became close friends and eventually fell in love. Calypso learned that sometimes, the best moments in life are the ones that don't involve any kind of excitement or thrill. The quiet moments spent with the people you love can be just as valuable and fulfilling.

Calypso and Alexander lived happily ever after, learning from each other and finding joy in their shared moments. Calypso had discovered a new kind of happiness, one that she had never known before, and she was grateful to Alexander for showing her the way.

Close your eyes and still the time around you. Can you feel the story coming alive within you? What do you need to alter to create a new experience? Allow yourself to be enveloped by the possibilities unfurling before you. What will you see? What will you feel in the depths of this new story?

Please write it down or stare at this empty page until it is filled with visions of magic, mystery and transformation.

Enjoy yourself!

26 THE LOVELY

Rumi was a very beautiful and attractive witch. People would stare at her everywhere she went in awe of her beauty. But what they didn't know was that Rumi was also incredibly smart and had a sharp mind.

Despite her intelligence, many people didn't take her seriously because they were too focused on her looks. They assumed that she was just a pretty face with nothing else to offer.

Rumi grew frustrated with this misconception and decided to prove everyone wrong. She began studying magic and ancient texts, using her sharp mind to uncover secrets that had been hidden for centuries.

As Rumi became more knowledgeable, she began to use her intelligence to help people. She would solve difficult problems and offer advice to those in need, all while still being as beautiful as ever.

Over time, people began to see Rumi in a different light. They realized that she was not just a pretty face but someone who was incredibly intelligent and capable. They respected her for her sharp mind and the many ways she used it to help others.

Rumi had proven that beauty and intelligence could go hand in hand. She showed the world that there was more to her than just her looks, and she was able to earn respect and admiration of those around her.

From that day on, Rumi continued to use her beauty and intelligence to help others. As a result, she became known as a powerful witch with a sharp mind, and people sought her out for her wisdom and guidance. And even though her looks still turned heads, her intelligence and kindness truly set her apart.

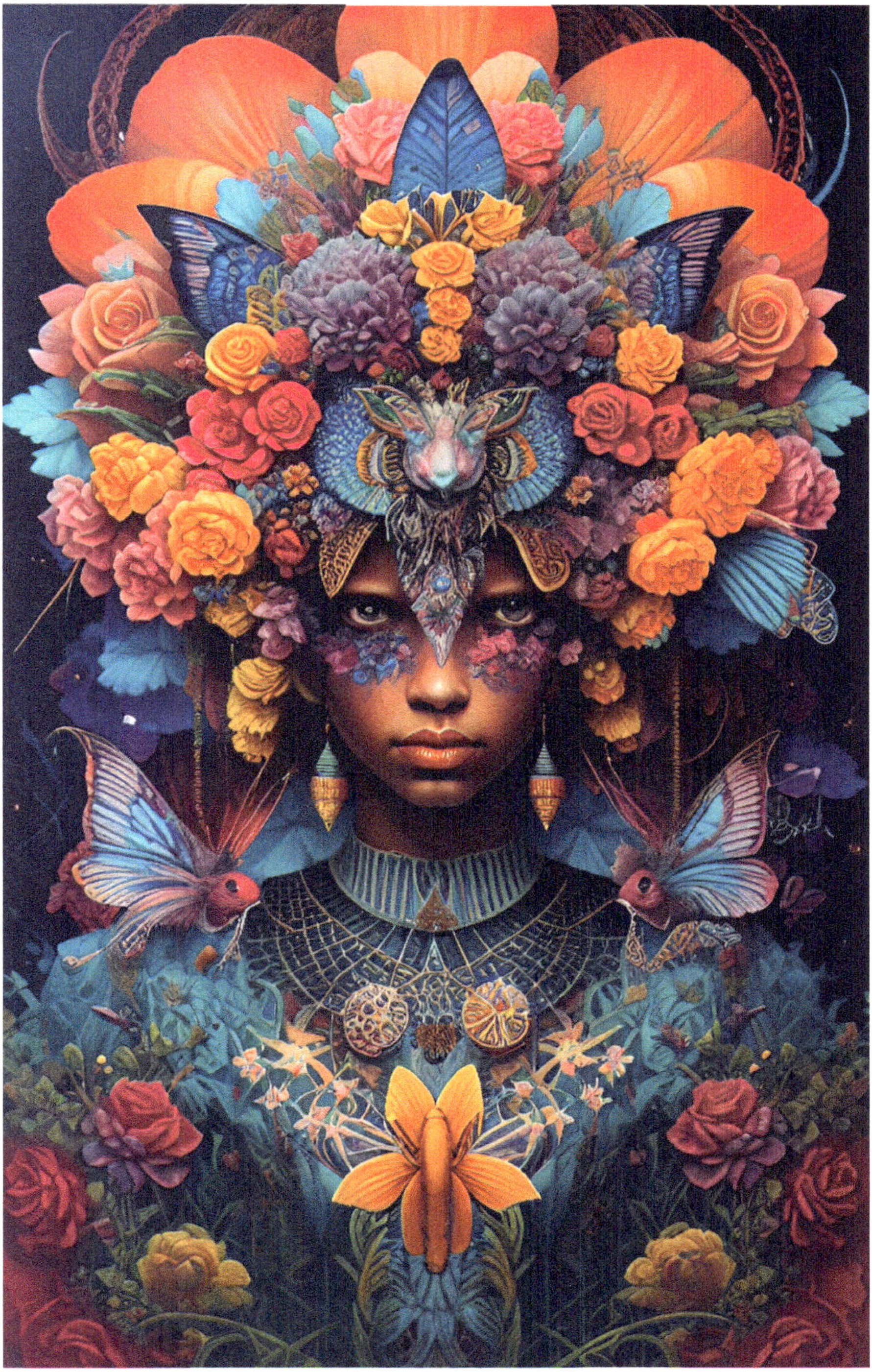

Close your eyes and still the time around you. Can you feel the story coming alive within you? What do you need to alter to create a new experience? Allow yourself to be enveloped by the possibilities unfurling before you. What will you see? What will you feel in the depths of this new story?

Please write it down or stare at this empty page until it is filled with visions of magic, mystery and transformation.

Enjoy yourself!

27 THE ENTERPRISING

Sappho was a beautiful, clever, and enterprising witch with a unique gift. As soon as she touched anything, it would instantly turn into gold. This made her the wealthiest witch in all the land, as she could turn even the simplest of things into precious treasure.

Sappho used her gift to start a successful business, turning ordinary objects into gold and selling them to the highest bidder. People came from all over the world to see her, marveling at her ability to turn anything into gold.

However, Sappho soon realized that her gift had a downside. She had become so focused on making money that she had lost sight of what was truly important. She had forgotten about her friends and family and the things that truly brought her happiness.

One day, Sappho's closest friend came to her, begging for her help. Her friend's daughter was sick, and the only way to save her was to find a rare herb that grew deep in the forest.

Sappho, being the enterprising witch that she was, immediately saw an opportunity. She offered to find the herb in exchange for a large sum of gold.

But as she journeyed into the forest, Sappho began to realize the true cost of her gift. She had become so focused on money that she had lost touch with the things that truly mattered. As she searched for the herb, she thought about all the people she had hurt in her quest for wealth.

When Sappho finally found the herb and returned it to her friend, she realized that she needed to make a change. She decided to use her gift for good rather than for her own selfish gain.

Sappho used her gift to help those in need, turning ordinary objects into gold and using the proceeds to help the less fortunate. She became known as a kind and generous witch, beloved by all who knew her.

And while she never lost her ability to turn things into gold, Sappho learned that there were more important things in life than wealth and material possessions. She rediscovered the joy of spending time with loved ones and the satisfaction that comes from doing good for others.

Close your eyes and still the time around you. Can you feel the story coming alive within you? What do you need to alter to create a new experience? Allow yourself to be enveloped by the possibilities unfurling before you. What will you see? What will you feel in the depths of this new story?

Please write it down or stare at this empty page until it is filled with visions of magic, mystery and transformation.

Enjoy yourself!

28 THE SELFLESS

Isaura was a beautiful, clever, and kind witch with a gold heart. She wanted nothing more than to save, comfort, and feed everyone she met. But unfortunately, she was constantly immersed in other people's worries and had forgotten everything about herself.

Isaura spent all of her time helping others, and she never took a moment for herself. She would travel to far-off lands to feed the hungry, heal the sick, and comfort the lonely. She gave away everything she had to help others, and she never once thought about her own needs.

Despite her best efforts, Isaura found that there were always more people in need. She began to feel overwhelmed, and she didn't know how to keep going.

One day, Isaura met an old woman who saw her right through. The woman told her that while it was good to help others, she couldn't do it at the expense of her own well-being. She urged Isaura to take care of herself, to rest, and to do the things that brought her joy.

At first, Isaura was hesitant. She didn't want to stop helping others, but the old woman's words had struck a chord with her. She realized that she couldn't keep giving and giving without taking care of herself first.

Isaura decided to take the old woman's advice. She began to take time for herself, to rest, to enjoy the simple pleasures of life, and to recharge her batteries.

As she rested and took care of herself, Isaura began to feel better. She found that she had more energy and was able to help others even more effectively than before.

But Isaura never forgot the lesson that the old woman had taught her. She made sure to always take care of herself first, prioritize her own needs, and find joy in the simple things.

Isaura continued to help others, but she did so with a newfound sense of balance and perspective. She knew that in order to make a real difference in the world, she needed to take care of herself first. And in doing so, she became an even more effective and powerful force for good.

Close your eyes and still the time around you. Can you feel the story coming alive within you? What do you need to alter to create a new experience? Allow yourself to be enveloped by the possibilities unfurling before you. What will you see? What will you feel in the depths of this new story?

Please write it down or stare at this empty page until it is filled with visions of magic, mystery and transformation.

Enjoy yourself!

29 ALTERING THE PAST

Veronica was a beautiful, clever, and lucky witch with a unique gift. She had the power to change the past. As soon as she focused her mind on a particular moment in time, she could alter the course of events and change the outcome of the past.

Veronica was careful with her power, knowing that changing the past could have unintended consequences. She only used her gift for good, helping those who had suffered from injustice or tragedy.

One day, Veronica was approached by a young woman who had lost her father in a tragic accident. The woman begged Veronica to use her gift to go back in time and save her father's life.

Veronica was hesitant. She knew that changing the past could have unintended consequences, and she was afraid of what might happen if she tried to save the young woman's father.

But the young woman was desperate, and Veronica couldn't ignore her pleas. She focused her mind on the moment of the accident and willed herself to go back in time. As she arrived at the scene of the accident, Veronica realized that she had arrived too late. She had missed the moment when she could have made a difference.

But Veronica was not one to give up easily. She continued to search for a way to change the past, traveling through time and space to find the key to saving the young woman's father.

Finally, after much searching, Veronica found what she was looking for. She discovered a moment in time when the accident could still have been prevented.

With all her power, Veronica willed the events to change. She watched as the accident was averted and the young woman's father was saved.

But as she returned to the present, Veronica realized that changing the past had come at a cost. The unintended consequences of her actions had caused ripples throughout time and space, and she had no way of knowing what the future would hold.

Veronica learned a valuable lesson that day. She realized that the past could not be changed without consequences and that sometimes it was best to let things play out as they were meant to. From that day on, she used her gift with caution, knowing that every action had a reaction and that sometimes the best course of action was to let the past be.

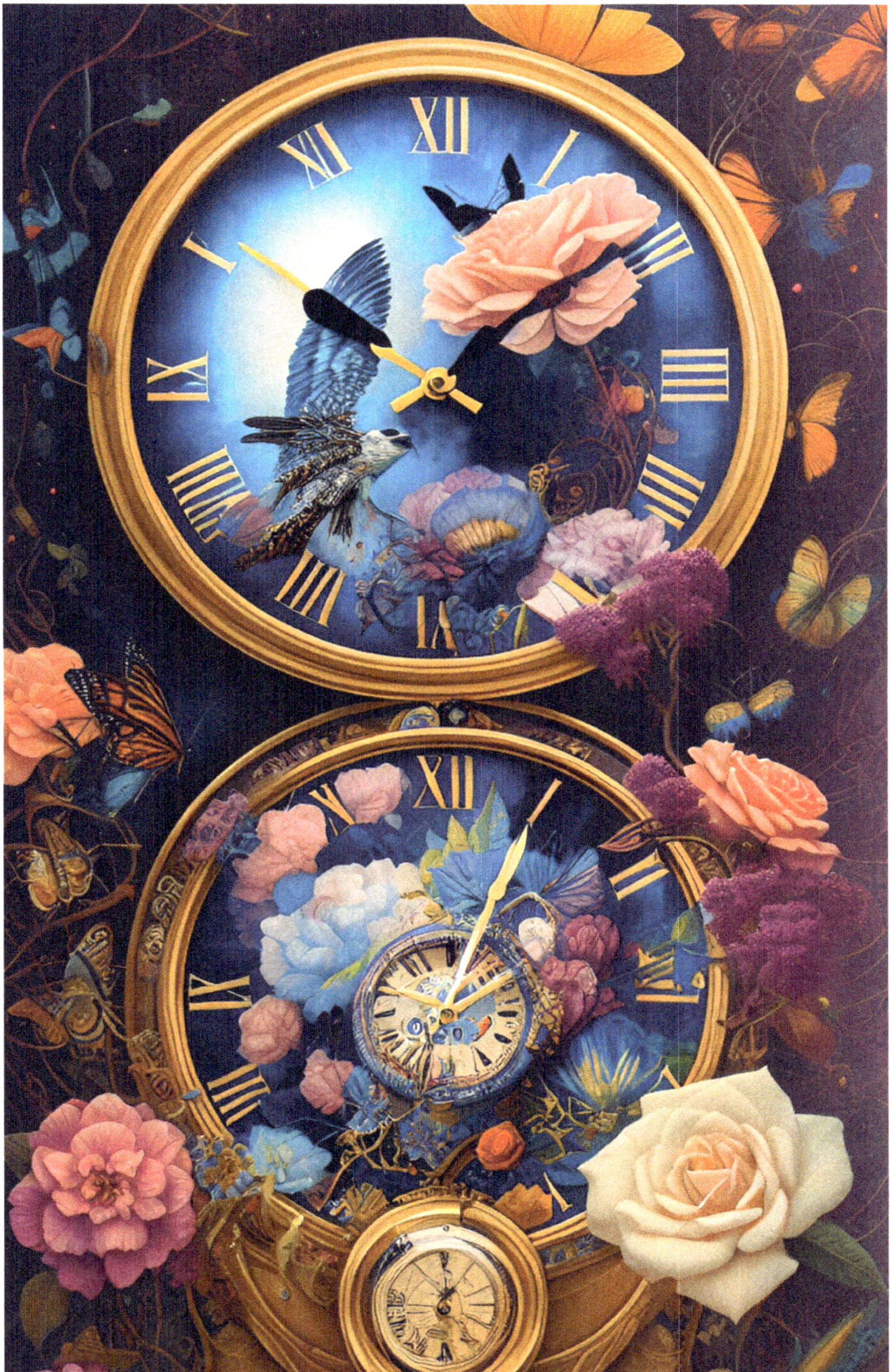

Close your eyes and still the time around you. Can you feel the story coming alive within you? What do you need to alter to create a new experience? Allow yourself to be enveloped by the possibilities unfurling before you. What will you see? What will you feel in the depths of this new story?

Please write it down or stare at this empty page until it is filled with visions of magic, mystery and transformation.

Enjoy yourself!

30 THE SCANDALIST

Once upon a time, in a magical kingdom, there was a beautiful and clever witch named Stephanie. She had a heart of gold and a mind that could solve any problem. However, she had a tendency to quarrel with the whole world and had trouble keeping friends. Stephanie had a sharp tongue and a quick temper. She was always ready to argue and fight, and her friends found it hard to be around her. She didn't understand why they couldn't see things her way, and she felt misunderstood and alone.

One day, Stephanie had a terrible argument with her closest friend, a gentle fairy named Lily. They said hurtful things to each other, and the friendship was broken beyond repair. Stephanie was devastated, but she didn't know how to make things right.

Stephanie began to realize that she had pushed away all her friends with her stubbornness and anger. She felt more alone than ever before, and she knew that something had to change. So, she set out on a journey to find a way to make amends and regain the trust of those she had hurt.

Stephanie traveled far and wide, facing dangers and overcoming obstacles. She met wise old sages and helpful animals who taught her valuable lessons about kindness and understanding. She began to understand that everyone had their own way of seeing the world and that listening and empathizing with others was important.

Stephanie also realized that she had to work on herself. She had to learn to control her temper and to be patient and understanding. It wasn't easy, but she was determined to become a better person.

As she journeyed, Stephanie encountered many people who had

been hurt by her in the past. She apologized and tried to make amends, but many were hesitant to forgive her. Stephanie didn't give up, though. She knew that it would take time to regain their trust and that she had to be patient and persistent.

As Stephanie continued on her journey, she began to see the world in a new light. She saw the beauty in the smallest things, and she began to appreciate the differences in people. She found that she was no longer quick to judge or criticize, but instead, she tried to understand and empathize with others.

Finally, after many months of travel, Stephanie returned to her home kingdom. She was no longer the same person that she had been before. She had learned valuable lessons about kindness, understanding, and forgiveness, and she was determined to make things right.

Stephanie sought out her old friends and apologized for her past behavior. She explained that she had been on a journey of self-discovery and that she had learned many important lessons. Slowly but surely, her friends began to forgive her, and Stephanie was overjoyed to have them back in her life.

Stephanie had finally found true friendship, and she knew that it was something that she would cherish for the rest of her life. She had learned that true friendship required patience, understanding, and forgiveness, and she was grateful for the lessons she had learned on her journey.

Close your eyes and still the time around you. Can you feel the story coming alive within you? What do you need to alter to create a new experience? Allow yourself to be enveloped by the possibilities unfurling before you. What will you see? What will you feel in the depths of this new story?

Please write it down or stare at this empty page until it is filled with visions of magic, mystery and transformation.

Enjoy yourself!

31 THE ANXIOUS

Once upon a time, there was a beautiful, intelligent, and sensitive witch named Nina. She was gifted with magical powers and had a keen mind that allowed her to solve any problem. However, Nina had a major problem - she was very anxious and worried about everything. Her heart was so tormented and her mind so frayed that she even forgot her way to the dream world and stopped sleeping.

Nina lived in a small cottage on the edge of the woods. She spent most of her time alone, tending to her garden and practicing her magic. She was known throughout the land as the most talented witch but also as the most anxious one. She could never sit still and was always worrying about something.

One day, Nina's anxiety became too much for her to handle. She stopped sleeping and couldn't remember how to find her way to the dream world. She tried everything she could think of, but nothing worked. Her anxiety only grew worse, and she was afraid that she would never sleep again.

Desperate for a solution, Nina sought out the help of a wise old owl who lived deep in the woods. The owl had a reputation for being able to solve even the most challenging problems, and Nina hoped that he could help her.

The owl listened carefully to Nina's story and soon realized that her anxiety was the root of her problem. He advised her to practice mindfulness and meditation to calm her mind and reduce her stress.

At first, Nina was hesitant. She had always been an anxious person and didn't think that meditation would help her. But with the owl's guidance, she began to practice mindfulness and meditation every day.

Slowly but surely, Nina's anxiety began to fade. She was able to sleep again and found that her mind was clearer and more focused than ever before. She was able to channel her magical powers more effectively, and her spells became even more potent.

Nina continued to practice mindfulness and meditation, and soon she was able to conquer her anxiety once and for all. She was able to enjoy life to the fullest, and she became known throughout the land as the most talented and peaceful witch.

As Nina looked back on her journey, she realized that she had learned a valuable lesson. She had learned that sometimes, the greatest magic is found within oneself. By conquering her anxiety, she unlocked her full potential and became the best version of herself.

And so, Nina continued to live in her small cottage on the edge of the woods, using her magic to help those in need. She had found true peace and happiness, and she knew that she would always be grateful for the lessons she had learned on her journey.

Close your eyes and still the time around you. Can you feel the story coming alive within you? What do you need to alter to create a new experience? Allow yourself to be enveloped by the possibilities unfurling before you. What will you see? What will you feel in the depths of this new story?

Please write it down or stare at this empty page until it is filled with visions of magic, mystery and transformation.

Enjoy yourself!

32 THE INDECISIVE

Once upon a time, in a magical kingdom, there was a beautiful and clever witch named Sophia. She had mastered all the knowledge, arts, and craftsmanship, and her skills were unparalleled. However, Sophia had a major problem - she could never make up her mind. She was plagued by the torment of choice and spent long hours in doubt.

Sophia lived in a grand castle filled with books, tools, and magical artifacts. She spent most of her time studying and practicing her crafts. She was known throughout the land as the most knowledgeable witch but also as the most indecisive one. She could never decide what to do or which path to take.

One day, Sophia was faced with a difficult decision. She had to choose between two powerful spells, both of which could help her in different ways. She spent hours agonizing over the decision, weighing the pros and cons of each spell. But the more she thought about it, the more confused she became.

Desperate for a solution, Sophia sought out the help of a wise old wizard who lived in a nearby cave. The wizard had a reputation for being able to solve even the most challenging problems, and Sophia hoped that he could help her.

The wizard listened carefully to Sophia's story and soon realized that her problem was not a lack of knowledge but rather an overabundance of it. Sophia had so many options that she couldn't make a decision.

The wizard advised Sophia to practice mindfulness and trust her instincts. He encouraged her to listen to her heart and to let go of her fears and doubts.

At first, Sophia was hesitant. She had always relied on her

knowledge and expertise to make decisions, and she didn't know if she could trust her instincts. But with the wizard's guidance, she began to practice mindfulness and let go of her fears and doubts.

Slowly but surely, Sophia's indecisiveness began to fade. She was able to make decisions more easily, and she found that her instincts were often right. She was able to use her magical skills more effectively, and her spells became even more potent.

Sophia continued to practice mindfulness and trust her instincts, and soon she was able to conquer her indecisiveness once and for all. She was able to enjoy life to the fullest, and she became known throughout the land as the most talented and decisive witch.

As Sophia looked back on her journey, she realized that she had learned a valuable lesson. She had learned that sometimes, the greatest knowledge is found within oneself. By trusting her instincts and letting go of her fears, she unlocked her full potential and became the best version of herself.

And so, Sophia continued to live in her grand castle, using her magic to help those in need. She had found true peace and happiness, and she knew that she would always be grateful for the lessons she had learned on her journey.

Close your eyes and still the time around you. Can you feel the story coming alive within you? What do you need to alter to create a new experience? Allow yourself to be enveloped by the possibilities unfurling before you. What will you see? What will you feel in the depths of this new story?

Please write it down or stare at this empty page until it is filled with visions of magic, mystery and transformation.

Enjoy yourself!

33 FOREVER YOUNG

Once upon a time, in a magical kingdom, there was a beautiful and clever witch named Anastasia. She had a heart of gold and a mind that could solve any problem. However, Anastasia had a major fear - she was very afraid to grow old.

Anastasia had been born with an immortal soul, and her beauty and youth never faded. She looked fresh and young, even as the years went by. But the thought of aging terrified her. She feared that she would lose her beauty and her magic would fade away.

Anastasia spent most of her time studying magic and looking for ways to stay young forever. She consulted ancient tomes, sought advice from other witches, and even experimented with powerful spells. But nothing worked, and her fear of growing old only grew stronger.

One day, Anastasia met a wise old sage who lived deep in the woods. The sage was ancient and wise, and he had a reputation for being able to solve even the most challenging problems. Anastasia hoped that he could help her.

The sage listened carefully to Anastasia's story and soon realized that her fear of growing old was not a problem of the body but rather a problem of the mind. He advised her to let go of her fear and to focus on living in the moment.

At first, Anastasia was hesitant. She had always been so focused on staying young that she didn't know how to let go of her fear. But with the sage's guidance, she began to focus on living in the present and enjoying every moment.

Anastasia began to appreciate the beauty of life and the wonder of the world around her. She found joy in the simplest things, like the sound of birdsong, the smell of flowers, and the touch of the sun on her skin. She began to realize that there was more to life than just youth and beauty.

As Anastasia let go of her fear, she found that her magic became even more potent. She was able to use her powers to help others in need and to spread joy and happiness throughout the land.

Years went by, and Anastasia grew older, but her beauty and magic never faded. She had learned to embrace the passage of time and to enjoy every moment of life. She had found true peace and happiness, and she knew that she would always be grateful for the lessons she had learned on her journey.

And so, Anastasia continued to live in her magical kingdom, spreading joy and happiness wherever she went. She had learned that true beauty and magic come from within and that the passing of time was just another part of the magic of life.

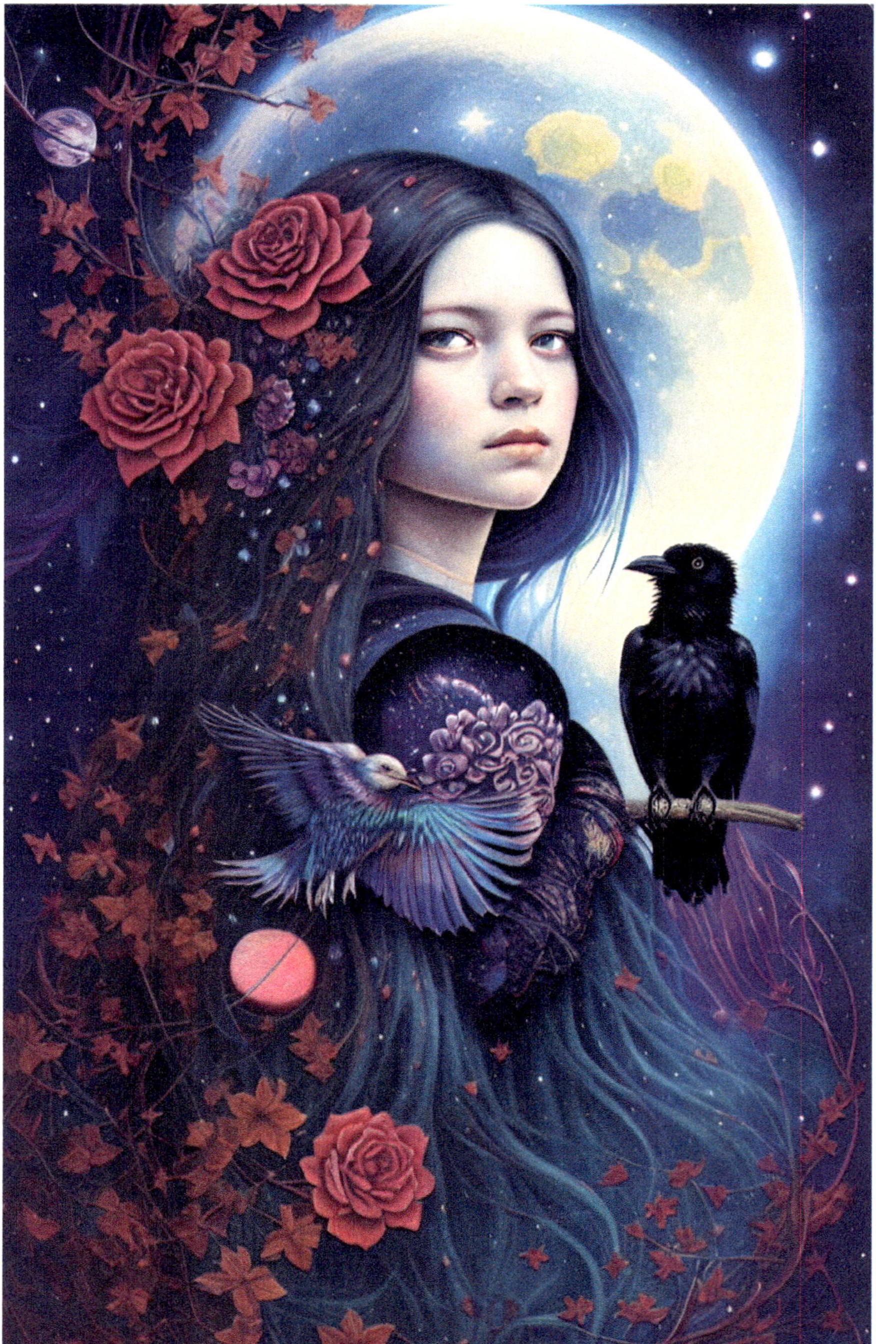

Close your eyes and still the time around you. Can you feel the story coming alive within you? What do you need to alter to create a new experience? Allow yourself to be enveloped by the possibilities unfurling before you. What will you see? What will you feel in the depths of this new story?

Please write it down or stare at this empty page until it is filled with visions of magic, mystery and transformation.

Enjoy yourself!

34 THE FEAR OF LOSS

Once upon a time, in a magical kingdom, there was a beautiful and clever witch named Sylvia. She had a heart of gold and a mind that could solve any problem. Sylvia was married to a very rich and fortunate man who loved her very much. Even though Sylvia was very happy, deep down, she was afraid that her husband might fall out of love with her.

Sylvia spent most of her time taking care of her husband and their home. She was a loving and devoted wife, but her fear of losing her husband's love consumed her thoughts. She worried that he might find someone else or that their love might fade away.

One day, Sylvia was out for a walk in the woods when she met a wise old owl. The owl had a reputation for being able to solve even the most challenging problems, and Sylvia hoped that he could help her.

The owl listened carefully to Sylvia's story and soon realized that her fear of losing her husband's love was not a problem of the heart but rather a problem of the mind. The wise man looked into Sylvia's eyes and said to her, "Fear is only as powerful as you allow it to be." He went on to explain that she should not let fear control her life. He told her that she had the power to choose how she wanted to live and love and that fear should not be a factor in making decisions. He advised her to let go of her fear and to focus on the present moment.

At first, Sylvia was hesitant. She had always been so focused on her husband's love that she didn't know how to let go of her fear. But with the owl's guidance, she began to focus on the present moment and to enjoy every moment with her husband.

Sylvia began to appreciate the love that she had and the wonder of the world around her. She found joy in the simplest things, like the sound of her husband's laughter, the taste of a good meal, and the feel of the sun on her skin. She began to realize that her fear was only holding her back and that there was more to life than just worrying about the future.

As Sylvia let go of her fear, she found that her love for her husband became even stronger. She was able to express her love more freely and enjoy every moment of their time together. She had learned to trust in the power of love and to appreciate the moments that they shared.

Years went by, and Sylvia and her husband grew older together, but their love never faded. They had learned to embrace the present moment and to enjoy every moment of life. They had found true peace and happiness, and they knew that they would always be grateful for the lessons they had learned on their journey.

And so, Sylvia continued to live in her magical kingdom with her husband, spreading joy and happiness wherever she went. She had learned that true love comes from within and that the passing of time was just another part of the magic of life.

Close your eyes and still the time around you. Can you feel the story coming alive within you? What do you need to alter to create a new experience? Allow yourself to be enveloped by the possibilities unfurling before you. What will you see? What will you feel in the depths of this new story?

Please write it down or stare at this empty page until it is filled with visions of magic, mystery and transformation.

Enjoy yourself!

35 THE LONELY

Once upon a time, a beautiful and clever witch named Samantha lived in a faraway kingdom. But despite her beauty and intelligence, no one seemed to love or appreciate her. This made Samantha sad and lonely, so she spent most of her days alone in the castle where she lived.

One day while wandering through the village market square looking for something to brighten up her spirits, she stumbled across an intriguing old woman selling trinkets from behind a special cloak with mysterious symbols embroidered.

The old woman noticed that Samantha looked very sad and smiled when asked what was wrong. Samantha explained how nobody loved or appreciated her. The old woman nodded knowingly before standing up. He said, "Sometimes all you need is just one person".

She told me about a powerful spell that can turn people's hearts if done correctly. The spell required lots of preparation and would take three nights, but it should solve your problem immediately after completion.

So without any more hesitation, the next night, Samantha began preparations for performing this unique magical ritual which involved reciting certain words and gathering rare ingredients like dragon scales, lilies of the valley, etc.

When all was ready on the third night at midnight, Samantha finished chanting incantations as instructed, conjuring out loud magical abilities gifted by gift goddesses, asking them to grant one wish that she desired most with all her heart.

Samantha wished for a companion who would have the same love and appreciation for her as she had longed to find. And so, at that exact moment, Azmir suddenly appeared in the room - a handsome yet mysterious prince from a distant kingdom. Azmir has been drawn by magical forces surrounding Samantha's ritual, sensing something special in this lonely woman he couldn't quite explain!

He was interested in watching this mysterious girl do what brought joy into hearts so fearlessly - dancing under moonlight every night! Slowly but surely, Azmir captivated Samantha's senses until neither could longer deny their connection.

It wasn't long before they two were happily together. Samantha had finally found the love she was searching for, and it seemed that Azmir had finally met his match in her! And so, with generous helpings of patience, understanding, and kindness as nourishment to their relationship, the two wise souls blossomed under stars that once made them feel so lonely.

Close your eyes and still the time around you. Can you feel the story coming alive within you? What do you need to alter to create a new experience? Allow yourself to be enveloped by the possibilities unfurling before you. What will you see? What will you feel in the depths of this new story?

Please write it down or stare at this empty page until it is filled with visions of magic, mystery and transformation.

Enjoy yourself!

36 SPEAKING TO THE WINDS

Once upon a time, in a magical kingdom, there was a beautiful and clever witch named Miranda. She had a heart of gold and a mind that could solve any problem. Miranda was always seeking her way among the stars, as everything seemed exciting and beautiful to her, and she couldn't make up her mind about where to go.

One day, Miranda decided to seek the guidance of the winds. She knew that the winds traveled far and wide, and she believed that they could help her find her way. She called upon the winds and asked them where she should go.

The winds responded in a whisper, "Follow your heart, dear Miranda, and it will guide you to your destination."

Miranda felt inspired by the winds' response and decided to set out on a journey to discover her true calling. She traveled far and wide, encountering many magical creatures and experiencing many wondrous adventures along the way.

One day, Miranda found herself in a beautiful meadow, surrounded by sparkling streams and colorful flowers. She sat down and closed her eyes, listening to the sounds of the wind rustling through the leaves of the trees.

As she sat there, she realized that the winds were right. She had been searching for her way among the stars, but all along, her heart had been guiding her to this very moment. She had found a place of peace and beauty where she could practice her magic and live a life filled with wonder and joy.

Miranda knew that this was where she was meant to be, and she spent the rest of her days in the meadow, practicing her magic and spreading joy and happiness to all who passed by. She had found her true calling, and she knew that she would always be grateful for the guidance of the winds.

And so, Miranda lived a life of magic and wonder, surrounded by the beauty of the natural world. She had learned that true happiness comes from following your heart and that the winds of fate will always guide you to where you are meant to be.

MONETA AGENCY

Close your eyes and still the time around you. Can you feel the story coming alive within you? What do you need to alter to create a new experience? Allow yourself to be enveloped by the possibilities unfurling before you. What will you see? What will you feel in the depths of this new story?

Please write it down or stare at this empty page until it is filled with visions of magic, mystery and transformation.

Enjoy yourself!

37 WAITING FOR SALVATION

Once upon a time, in a magical kingdom, there was a beautiful and clever witch named Esther. She had a heart of gold and a mind that could solve any problem. Esther was held captive by old dreams and was waiting for someone to rescue her, but no one came.

Esther had spent most of her life dreaming of a grand adventure, where she would travel far and wide, encountering magical creatures and solving great mysteries. She was waiting for someone to come and sweep her off her feet, to take her away from the mundane world and into a life of adventure.

Years went by, and Esther's dreams remained unfulfilled. She was held captive by the idea that someone would come and rescue her, that her life would suddenly become a grand adventure. But no one came.

One day, Esther realized that she had been waiting for too long. She knew that if she wanted her dreams to come true, she would have to make them happen herself. She decided to take matters into her own hands and set out on a journey to fulfill her own destiny.

Esther traveled far and wide, encountering many challenges and obstacles along the way. But she never gave up, and she never lost faith in her dreams. She knew that she was capable of achieving great things, and she was determined to make her dreams a reality.

As she journeyed on, Esther discovered that the greatest adventure of all was the journey of self-discovery. She learned that true happiness and fulfillment came from within, and that the only way to achieve her dreams was to believe in herself and to never give up.

And so, Esther continued on her journey, becoming stronger and wiser with every step. She had broken free from the captivity of old dreams and had embraced a life of adventure and self-discovery. She knew that the road ahead would be long and challenging, but she was ready to face it head-on, with courage and determination.

Esther had learned that the power to create her own destiny was within her all along, and she would never forget the lesson she had learned on her journey. She knew that she would always be grateful for the adventure that had set her free.

Close your eyes and still the time around you. Can you feel the story coming alive within you? What do you need to alter to create a new experience? Allow yourself to be enveloped by the possibilities unfurling before you. What will you see? What will you feel in the depths of this new story?

Please write it down or stare at this empty page until it is filled with visions of magic, mystery and transformation.

Enjoy yourself!

38 THE IMMORTAL

Once upon a time, in a magical kingdom, there was a beautiful, clever, and insightful witch named Karin. She had a heart of gold and a mind that could solve any problem. Karin had always been fascinated by the idea of immortality and had searched for a way to achieve it. But one day, she learned that true immortality could only be gained by learning to live in the present.

Karin decided to let go of her past and stop worrying about the future. She began to focus on the present moment, feeling the blood flowing through her veins and the electricity running through her nerves. She discovered that every moment was an eternity to her and that the present held all the magic and wonder she could ever need.

As Karin learned to live in the present, she discovered that true immortality was not about living forever but about living fully. She began to appreciate the beauty of life and the wonder of the world around her. She found joy in the simplest things, like the sound of birdsong, the feel of the sun on her skin, and the taste of a good meal.

Karin's newfound wisdom brought her great joy and inner peace. She no longer feared death or worried about the future. She knew that every moment was a gift, and she treasured each one as if it were her last.

As the years went by, Karin's beauty and magic never faded. She had learned to embrace the passage of time and to enjoy every moment of life. She had found true peace and happiness, and she knew that she would always be grateful for the lessons she had learned on her journey.

And so, Karin lived on in her magical kingdom, spreading joy and happiness wherever she went. She had learned that true immortality comes from within and that the present moment holds all the magic and wonder we could ever need. Karin had found true happiness by living in the present, and she knew that she would always be grateful for the gift of immortality that came from within.

Close your eyes and still the time around you. Can you feel the story coming alive within you? What do you need to alter to create a new experience? Allow yourself to be enveloped by the possibilities unfurling before you. What will you see? What will you feel in the depths of this new story?

Please write it down or stare at this empty page until it is filled with visions of magic, mystery and transformation.

Enjoy yourself!

39 MOTHER'S DAUGHTER

Once upon a time, in a magical kingdom, there was a beautiful and clever witch named Charlotte. Despite her wisdom and knowledge, Charlotte continued to be afraid of her mother, even as an adult.

Charlotte's mother had always been a source of anxiety and stress for her. She had grown up in a home where her mother's words and actions had a powerful impact on her. No matter how much Charlotte tried to overcome her fear, it seemed to hold her back.

One day, Charlotte decided that she had had enough. She knew that she needed to confront her fear and overcome it once and for all. She summoned all her courage and went to see her mother.

At first, the conversation was difficult, as Charlotte struggled to express her feelings. But as they talked, she began to realize that her mother's actions were not a reflection of her love for her but rather a reflection of her own fears and insecurities.

Charlotte's mother opened up to her, and together they began to work through their issues. They discovered that their relationship was not defined by fear but by a deep and abiding love that had always been there.

As Charlotte confronted her fear and worked through her issues, she discovered that she was stronger than she had ever imagined. She found that her love for her mother was not defined by fear but by a deep and abiding connection that would always be a part of her.

From that day on, Charlotte lived her life with a renewed sense of purpose and confidence. She had confronted her fears and overcome them, and she knew that she was capable of anything she set her mind to. She had learned that love could conquer fear and that true strength came from within.

And so, Charlotte continued to live in her magical kingdom, spreading love and joy wherever she went. She had learned that fear was not something to be ashamed of but rather something to be conquered with love and understanding. Charlotte had found true peace and happiness, and she knew that she would always be grateful for the lessons she had learned on her journey.

MONETA AGENCY

Close your eyes and still the time around you. Can you feel the story coming alive within you? What do you need to alter to create a new experience? Allow yourself to be enveloped by the possibilities unfurling before you. What will you see? What will you feel in the depths of this new story?

Please write it down or stare at this empty page until it is filled with visions of magic, mystery and transformation.

Enjoy yourself!

40 THE LOST

Once upon a time, in a magical kingdom, there was a curious and rebellious witch named Mae. Mae loved to explore the world, and she often went on adventures that took her far from home. One day, Mae strayed so far from home that she couldn't find her way back.

Feeling lost and alone, Mae asked the world for five clues that would help her find her way home. The first clue came to her in the form of a beautiful rainbow that appeared in the sky. Mae knew that rainbows always pointed to a new beginning, and she took this as a sign that she needed to start fresh and try a new path.

The second clue came in the form of a friendly bird that flew down to her and chirped a happy tune. Mae knew that birds were often a symbol of freedom, and she took this as a sign that she needed to let go of her fears and trust in her own abilities.

The third clue came to Mae in the form of a beautiful flower that bloomed in her path. She knew that flowers often represented growth and renewal, and she took this as a sign that she needed to open herself up to new experiences and opportunities.

The fourth clue came to Mae in the form of a kind stranger who stopped to help her. Mae knew that kindness was a powerful force, and she took this as a sign that she needed to be more compassionate and understanding toward others.

The fifth and final clue came to Mae in the form of a wise old tree that stood tall and strong in the forest. Mae knew that trees were often a symbol of wisdom and resilience, and she took this as a sign that she needed to be patient and strong as she made her way home.

As Mae followed the five clues, she began to feel a sense of hope and purpose. She knew that she would find her way home and that her adventures had taught her valuable lessons about herself and the world around her.

Eventually, Mae found her way back home, but she was forever changed by her journey. She knew that the world was full of wonder and beauty, but she also knew that it could be a dangerous and unpredictable place. Mae had learned to be brave and resourceful, and she knew that she would always be grateful for the five clues that had brought her home.

Close your eyes and still the time around you. Can you feel the story coming alive within you? What do you need to alter to create a new experience? Allow yourself to be enveloped by the possibilities unfurling before you. What will you see? What will you feel in the depths of this new story?

Please write it down or stare at this empty page until it is filled with visions of magic, mystery and transformation.

Enjoy yourself!

41 THE MOTHER BIRD

Once upon a time, in a magical kingdom, there was a sensitive and perceptive witch named Loni. She had a heart of gold and a mind that could solve any problem. Loni was a loving mother to her children, but she was always worrying about them.

She worried about their safety, their health, and their happiness. She worried about every little thing, and her worries consumed her thoughts and her energy. But Loni knew that her worries were not helping her children and that she needed to find a way to overcome her fears.

One day, Loni decided to seek the advice of a wise old wizard who lived in a distant land. She set out on a journey to find the wizard, hoping that he could help her overcome her worries and fears.

As she journeyed on, Loni encountered many challenges and obstacles, but she never gave up. She knew that she needed to find a way to overcome her fears and worries if she was to be the best mother she could be.

Finally, Loni arrived at the wizard's tower, and she told him all about her worries and fears. The wise old wizard listened carefully, and then he told her a story.

He told her about a mother bird who was always worrying about her baby bird. The mother bird was so worried that the baby bird would fall out of the nest that she never gave the baby bird a chance to learn to fly. But one day, the baby bird decided to take a leap of faith and spread its wings. And to the mother bird's amazement, the baby bird flew high and soared through the sky.

The wizard told Loni that she needed to let her children spread their wings and learn to fly. She needed to trust in their abilities and give them the space they needed to grow and explore the world around them.

Loni realized that the wizard was right, and she returned home with a renewed sense of purpose and confidence. She began to let go of her worries and fears, and she started to trust in her children's abilities.

As Loni's children grew and flourished, she saw that they were capable of achieving great things. She had learned to let go of her worries and fears, and she had discovered the true power of trust and faith.

And so, Loni continued to live in her magical kingdom, spreading love and joy wherever she went. She had learned that the true mark of a great mother was not how much she worried but how much she loved and trusted in her children's abilities. Loni had found true peace and happiness, and she knew that she would always be grateful for the lessons she had learned on her journey.

Close your eyes and still the time around you. Can you feel the story coming alive within you? What do you need to alter to create a new experience? Allow yourself to be enveloped by the possibilities unfurling before you. What will you see? What will you feel in the depths of this new story?

Please write it down or stare at this empty page until it is filled with visions of magic, mystery and transformation.

Enjoy yourself!

42 THE PHONY

Once upon a time, in a magical kingdom, there was a beautiful witch named Nadine. She had a heart of gold and a mind that could weave the most enchanting tales. Nadine was known as the best storyteller in the world, and people came from far and wide to hear her stories.

However, despite the joy that her stories brought to people's hearts, they thought they were all untrue. They believed that Nadine had made them up, that they were nothing more than figments of her imagination.

Nadine knew that her stories were true, but she wanted to prove it to all of her listeners. She decided to set out on a journey to find the magical creatures and places that she had described in her stories.

As she journeyed on, Nadine encountered many challenges and obstacles, but she never gave up. She knew that she needed to find a way to prove the truth of her stories if she was to be believed.

Finally, Nadine arrived at a magical forest where she had said that unicorns roamed. She set out to find them, and to her amazement, she did. She saw the unicorns with her own eyes, and she knew that her stories were true.

Nadine continued on her journey, visiting all the magical creatures and places that she had described in her stories. She saw fairies, dragons, and mermaids, and she knew that her stories were not just figments of her imagination.

When she returned to her kingdom, Nadine told her listeners about her journey, and she showed them the evidence she had gathered along the way. They were amazed and delighted, and they knew that her stories were true.

From that day on, Nadine continued to tell her stories, and people listened to them with a new appreciation and wonder. They knew that her stories were not just tales but real experiences that she had had on her journey.

And so, Nadine continued to live in her magical kingdom, spreading love and joy wherever she went. She had proven the truth of her stories, and she had shown people that magic and wonder truly existed in the world. Nadine had found true peace and happiness, and she knew that she would always be grateful for the lessons she had learned on her journey.

MONETA AGENCY

Close your eyes and still the time around you. Can you feel the story coming alive within you? What do you need to alter to create a new experience? Allow yourself to be enveloped by the possibilities unfurling before you. What will you see? What will you feel in the depths of this new story?

Please write it down or stare at this empty page until it is filled with visions of magic, mystery and transformation.

Enjoy yourself!

43 A SEEKER OF VIVID IMPRESSIONS

Once upon a time, in a magical kingdom, there was a charming and perceptive witch named Kim. She had a heart of gold and a mind that could charm anyone. Kim made friends very easily and quickly, and she was known for her social prowess.

However, when it came to romantic relationships, Kim was different. She indiscriminately got involved in relationships and just as quickly lost interest in them. She moved from one partner to another, never truly connecting with anyone.

One day, Kim met a handsome prince named William. She was immediately drawn to him, and they started dating. However, as time went on, Kim began to lose interest in William. She didn't feel the same spark that she had felt in the beginning, and she started to distance herself from him.

William was hurt and confused, but he didn't give up on their relationship. He knew that Kim was a special person, and he wanted to understand her better. He decided to ask her about her past relationships, hoping to gain some insight into her behavior.

Kim opened up to William, telling him about her fears of commitment and her need for constant excitement and new experiences. William listened carefully, and he knew that he could help her overcome her fears.

He took Kim on a journey to a magical land where they could experience all kinds of exciting and new things. They went on adventures, explored new places, and tried new foods. William showed Kim that there was excitement and adventure in every moment and that they didn't need to constantly seek out new experiences to be happy.

As Kim began to open up to William and let go of her fears, she started to see him in a new light. She saw that he was a kind and caring person, and she knew that he was the one for her.

From that day on, Kim and William continued to live in the magical kingdom, spreading love and joy wherever they went. Kim had learned that true happiness comes from within and that she didn't need to constantly seek out new experiences to be happy. She had found true peace and happiness with William, and she knew that she would always be grateful for the lessons she had learned on her journey.

Close your eyes and still the time around you. Can you feel the story coming alive within you? What do you need to alter to create a new experience? Allow yourself to be enveloped by the possibilities unfurling before you. What will you see? What will you feel in the depths of this new story?

Please write it down or stare at this empty page until it is filled with visions of magic, mystery and transformation.

Enjoy yourself!

44 THE WRONG

Once upon a time, in a magical kingdom, there was a sweet and pretty witch named Molly. She had a heart of gold and a mind that loved to make mistakes. She knew that mistakes were part of the journey of life, and she never let them bring her down.

Molly loved to try new things, and she was always curious about the world around her. She wasn't afraid to take risks and make mistakes, knowing that each mistake would lead her on a new and exciting path.

One day, Molly accidentally mixed up a potion that turned her hair bright purple. At first, she was embarrassed and upset, but then she realized that her new look was fun and unique. People started to take notice of her, and she felt more confident and alive than ever before.

As Molly continued to make mistakes, each one changed the trajectory of her life. One mistake led her to discover a hidden talent for singing, and she became a beloved performer in the kingdom. Another mistake led her to meet her true love, a handsome prince who fell in love with her purple hair and adventurous spirit.

Through all of her mistakes, Molly never lost her sense of wonder and joy. She knew that each mistake was a new opportunity to learn and grow, and she welcomed them with open arms.

As she continued on her journey, Molly became known as the "Mistake Witch." People came from all over the kingdom to hear her stories of how her mistakes had led her to new and exciting adventures.

And so, Molly continued to live in the magical kingdom,

spreading love and joy wherever she went. She had learned that mistakes were not something to be feared or avoided but something to be embraced and celebrated. Molly had found true peace and happiness, and she knew that she would always be grateful for the lessons she had learned on her journey.

Close your eyes and still the time around you. Can you feel the story coming alive within you? What do you need to alter to create a new experience? Allow yourself to be enveloped by the possibilities unfurling before you. What will you see? What will you feel in the depths of this new story?

Please write it down or stare at this empty page until it is filled with visions of magic, mystery and transformation.

Enjoy yourself!

45 THE FORGOTTEN NAME

Once upon a time, in a magical kingdom, there was a beautiful and talented witch named Hadwig. She had a heart of gold and a mind that could create the most enchanting spells. Hadwig was known throughout the kingdom for her extraordinary talent and her beautiful spirit.

One day, while on her way to a magic tournament, Hadwig suddenly forgot her own name. She couldn't remember who she was, where she was going, or what she was supposed to do. She was overcome with fear and confusion, and she didn't know how to continue.

Hadwig stumbled through the kingdom, trying to find anyone who could help her. She asked every witch, wizard, and fairy she met if they knew her name, but no one could help her.

As time went on, Hadwig's condition only worsened. She became more and more disoriented, and she couldn't remember even the simplest spells. She was becoming a shell of her former self, and she didn't know how to escape the darkness that had taken over her mind.

Finally, Hadwig came across a wise old wizard who lived in a distant land. The wizard listened carefully to her story, and he knew that he could help her. He told her that in order to remember her name, she needed to remember who she truly was.

The wizard took Hadwig on a journey through the kingdom, showing her all of the places where she had created her most beautiful spells. He reminded her of the people she had helped, the magic she had created, and the love she had spread.

As Hadwig began to remember her true self, her name came back to her. She felt a sense of relief and joy wash over her, and she knew that she could finally return to her life as a beautiful and talented witch.

And so, Hadwig returned to the kingdom, spreading love and joy wherever she went. She had learned that the most important thing was not her name but the beauty and magic that she brought into the world. Hadwig had found true peace and happiness, and she knew that she would always be grateful for the lessons she had learned on her journey.

MONETA AGENCY

Close your eyes and still the time around you. Can you feel the story coming alive within you? What do you need to alter to create a new experience? Allow yourself to be enveloped by the possibilities unfurling before you. What will you see? What will you feel in the depths of this new story?

Please write it down or stare at this empty page until it is filled with visions of magic, mystery and transformation.

Enjoy yourself!

46 THE DEFENDER

Once upon a time, in a magical kingdom, there was a beautiful and clever witch named Ginger. She had a heart of gold and a mind that could create the most powerful spells. But what made Ginger truly special was her unique ability to transform into a bird.

Ginger loved to fly through the skies as a bird, soaring high above the clouds and feeling the wind rush through her feathers. She would fly through the forest, over the mountains, and through the valleys, exploring the world from a bird's-eye view.

One day, while flying over the kingdom, Ginger noticed that the people below were in trouble. A group of trolls had invaded the kingdom, and they were wreaking havoc everywhere they went. The people were scared and didn't know what to do.

Ginger knew that she had to help. She quickly transformed into a bird and flew down to the kingdom, determined to stop the trolls and save the day.

As she soared through the air, Ginger began to cast powerful spells, turning the trolls into harmless creatures and sending them running in fear. She protected the people of the kingdom, and they were amazed at the power and beauty of the bird that had come to their aid.

Ginger continued to fly through the kingdom, keeping an eye out for any trouble that might arise. She would transform into a bird whenever she needed to, swooping down to stop any danger that came her way.

As time went on, Ginger became known as the "Bird Witch." People would look up to the sky whenever they needed help, knowing that Ginger would be there to protect them. She had found a new purpose in life, and she knew that she would always be grateful for the lessons she had learned on her journey.

And so, Ginger continued to fly through the kingdom, spreading love and joy wherever she went. She had learned that her unique ability to transform into a bird was a gift that she could use to protect and help others. Ginger had found true peace and happiness, and she knew that she would always be grateful for the lessons she had learned on her journey.

Close your eyes and still the time around you. Can you feel the story coming alive within you? What do you need to alter to create a new experience? Allow yourself to be enveloped by the possibilities unfurling before you. What will you see? What will you feel in the depths of this new story?

Please write it down or stare at this empty page until it is filled with visions of magic, mystery and transformation.

Enjoy yourself!

47 THE WORLD CHANGER

Once upon a time, in a magical kingdom, there was a beautiful and willful witch named Esme. She had a heart of gold and a mind that could create the most enchanting spells. But what made Esme truly special was her desire to change the world.

Esme looked around the kingdom and saw that there was so much suffering and pain. She knew that she had the power to make a difference, and she was determined to use her magic to make the world a better place.

Esme cast a powerful spell that created a beautiful garden full of lush flowers and fragrant herbs. The garden became a sanctuary for the people of the kingdom, a place where they could find peace and happiness.

Esme continued to create new spells and magic, each one more powerful and beautiful than the last. She used her magic to heal the sick, protect the weak, and spread love and joy throughout the kingdom.

As Esme continued to change the world with her magic, people began to take notice. They saw the beauty and power of her spells, and they knew that she was a true force for good in the world.

But there were some who were threatened by Esme's power. They saw her as a threat to their own control over the kingdom, and they began to plot against her.

One day, Esme was ambushed by a group of witches who wanted to take her down. But Esme was too powerful for them. She cast a spell that created a whirlwind of magic, sweeping the witches away and protecting herself from harm.

From that day on, Esme became known as the "Willful Witch."

People looked up to her as a symbol of hope and strength, knowing that she would always fight for what was right and just.

And so, Esme continued to change the world with her magic, spreading love and joy wherever she went. Finally, she had found her purpose in life, and she knew that she would always be grateful for the lessons she had learned on her journey. Esme had found true peace and happiness, and she knew that she would always be remembered as one of the greatest witches to ever live.

Close your eyes and still the time around you. Can you feel the story coming alive within you? What do you need to alter to create a new experience? Allow yourself to be enveloped by the possibilities unfurling before you. What will you see? What will you feel in the depths of this new story?

Please write it down or stare at this empty page until it is filled with visions of magic, mystery and transformation.

Enjoy yourself!

48 THE SPOTLIGHTED

Once upon a time, in a magical kingdom, there was a beautiful witch named Cassandra. She had a heart of gold and a mind that could create the most powerful spells. But what made Cassandra truly unique was that she was invisible.

Being invisible gave Cassandra many advantages. She could go anywhere without being seen, and she could hear and see things that others couldn't. She was able to help people in secret, without them even knowing that she was there.

But despite all of the advantages of being invisible, Cassandra still longed to be visible. She wanted to be seen, to be heard, and to be recognized for the good work that she did in the world.

One day, Cassandra met a wise old wizard who lived deep in the forest. The wizard listened carefully to her story and knew exactly what she needed. He gave her a potion that would allow her to become visible for just one day.

Cassandra was overjoyed. She drank the potion and felt her body tingle as she began to appear before her eyes. She looked down and saw her hands, her feet, and her clothes all visible for the first time.

Cassandra spent the day exploring the kingdom, seeing everything with new eyes. She visited the people she had helped in secret, revealing herself to them and seeing their joy and gratitude in person.

As the day drew to a close, Cassandra felt a sadness creeping in. She knew that her time as a visible witch was coming to an end, and she didn't want to go back to being invisible.

But the wise old wizard had one more surprise for her. He told her that, although she could not always be visible, she could always be seen. He reminded her that the people she had helped knew that she was there, even if they couldn't see her. They felt her love and her magic, and they knew that she was a true force for good in the world.

And so, Cassandra went back to being invisible, but with a newfound sense of purpose and joy. She knew that she was making a difference in the world, and that was all that mattered. Cassandra had found true peace and happiness, and she knew that she would always be grateful for the lessons she had learned on her journey.

MONETA AGENCY

Close your eyes and still the time around you. Can you feel the story coming alive within you? What do you need to alter to create a new experience? Allow yourself to be enveloped by the possibilities unfurling before you. What will you see? What will you feel in the depths of this new story?

Please write it down or stare at this empty page until it is filled with visions of magic, mystery and transformation.

Enjoy yourself!

49 ROSES AGAINST THE WIND

Once upon a time, in a magical kingdom, there was a beautiful witch named Susan. She had a heart of gold and a mind that could create the most enchanting spells. But what made Susan truly special was her love for the wind.

Every day, Susan would go out into her beautiful garden and feel the wind rushing through her hair. She would close her eyes and let the wind take her on a journey to distant lands, experiencing the wonders of the world in a way that no one else could.

But one day, as Susan was flying with the wind, something strange happened. The wind disappeared, leaving Susan in an unfamiliar area far from home. She looked around, but she had no idea where she was.

Susan tried to find her way back home, but she wandered for days, growing tired and exhausted. She was lost and alone, and she didn't know what to do.

After many years of getting lost, Susan's beautiful garden began to fall into disrepair. The roses she had once tended with such care were now overgrown and unkempt, and she knew that she needed to do something to save them.

One day, as she was tending to her garden, the roses came to life. They twisted and turned, creating a labyrinth in which the wind would get tangled if it flew into the garden. The roses knew that if they could stop the wind from taking Susan away, she would be able to tend to the garden and keep it beautiful once again.

The wind flew into the garden, as it had so many times before, but this time it was different. It became tangled in the labyrinth of roses, unable to escape. Susan watched in amazement as the roses worked their magic, protecting her from the wind that she loved so much.

From that day on, Susan's garden flourished once again. She tended to the roses with care and love, and the garden became more beautiful than it had ever been before. The roses had saved her, and she was grateful for their kindness and magic.

And so, Susan continued to love the wind, but she knew that the roses were there to protect her if she ever needed it. She had found her way back home, and she knew that she would always be grateful for the lessons she had learned on her journey. Susan had found true peace and happiness, and she knew that she would always be remembered as one of the greatest witches to ever live.

Close your eyes and still the time around you. Can you feel the story coming alive within you? What do you need to alter to create a new experience? Allow yourself to be enveloped by the possibilities unfurling before you. What will you see? What will you feel in the depths of this new story?

Please write it down or stare at this empty page until it is filled with visions of magic, mystery and transformation.

Enjoy yourself!

50 THE HEALING FOOD

Once upon a time, in a magical kingdom, there was a beautiful and talented witch named Ursula. She had a heart of gold and a mind that could create the most enchanting spells. But what made Ursula truly unique was her love for cooking.

Ursula was a master chef who knew how to mix flavors in ways that no one else could. She would mix spicy and sweet, tart and viscous, salty and sour, creating new flavors that left people speechless. People from all over the world came to taste her food, knowing that it would heal the wounds of their hearts, revive their faded feelings, and restore their courage.

Ursula's kitchen was always bustling with activity. She had magical pots and pans, enchanted spoons and knives, and a vast collection of rare and exotic ingredients that she had gathered from all over the world. Her kitchen was a place of wonder and enchantment, a place where dreams were born, and magic was made.

One day, a young woman named Sophia came to Ursula's kitchen. Sophia had lost her way in life and was looking for something to help her find her way back. She had heard about Ursula's magical food and knew that it was just what she needed.

Ursula welcomed Sophia into her kitchen and began to prepare a feast for her. She mixed spices and herbs, sprinkled them with fairy dust, and whispered magical incantations over the pots and pans. As the food cooked, the air was filled with the most enchanting scents, and Sophia's heart began to lift.

When the food was ready, Ursula served it to Sophia. She took a bite, and her taste buds were transported to a new world of flavor and magic. The food was like nothing she had ever tasted before, and she knew that it was exactly what she needed to find her way back to herself.

Ursula's food had a magical power that healed Sophia's heart, restored her courage, and revived her faded feelings. Sophia felt like a new person, full of hope and wonder, and she knew that she would never forget the magic of Ursula's kitchen.

And so, Ursula continued to create her magical food, healing hearts and bringing joy to people all over the world. Her kitchen became a place of wonder and enchantment, a place where dreams were born, and magic was made. Ursula had found her purpose in life, and she knew that she would always be grateful for the lessons she had learned on her journey.

Close your eyes and still the time around you. Can you feel the story coming alive within you? What do you need to alter to create a new experience? Allow yourself to be enveloped by the possibilities unfurling before you. What will you see? What will you feel in the depths of this new story?

Please write it down or stare at this empty page until it is filled with visions of magic, mystery and transformation.

Enjoy yourself!

51 THE STUBBORN HEART

Once upon a time, in a magical kingdom, there was a beautiful and perceptive witch named Nancy. She had a heart of gold, but her heart had a mind of its own. It would beat when it wanted to and stop when it got upset, causing Nancy great anxiety and worry.

One day, Nancy decided that she was tired of her willful heart, and she set out on a journey to learn how to control it. She traveled far and wide, searching for a solution to her problem. She asked everyone she met for help, but no one had the answer she was looking for.

Finally, Nancy came across a wise old wizard who told her that the key to controlling her heart was to cheat it. He explained that if she could trick her heart into thinking that it was happy and content, it would beat steadily and smoothly.

Nancy was intrigued and asked the wizard how she could cheat her heart. The wizard told her that the only way to do it was to fill her life with joy and wonder. He told her to seek out the things that made her happy and to surround herself with people who brought her joy.

Nancy took the wizard's advice and began to live her life with joy and wonder. She danced in the rain, explored the forests, and chased the stars. She surrounded herself with people who made her happy and learned to see the magic in everything.

As she filled her life with joy and wonder, Nancy felt her heart begin to beat steadily and smoothly. It no longer stopped when it was upset or beat too quickly when it was happy. It had become content and happy, just like Nancy.

And so, Nancy had learned to cheat her heart and to control

it. She had found happiness and joy in the simplest of things and had learned to appreciate the magic of life. Her heart beat steadily and smoothly, bringing her peace and contentment.

From that day on, Nancy lived her life with joy and wonder, seeking out the things that made her happy and surrounding herself with people who brought her joy. She had learned the secret to a happy heart, and she knew that she would always be grateful for the lessons she had learned on her journey.

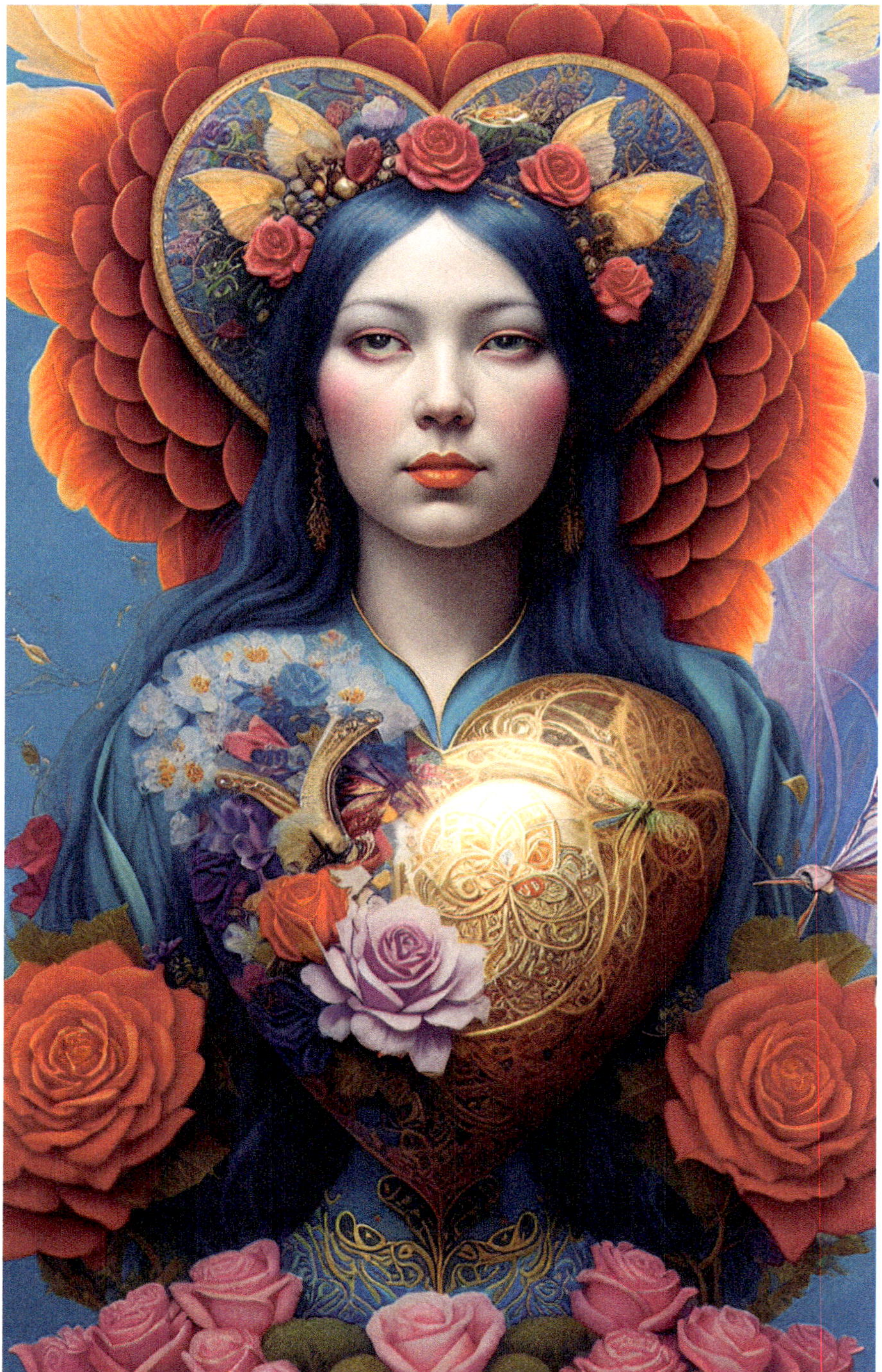

Close your eyes and still the time around you. Can you feel the story coming alive within you? What do you need to alter to create a new experience? Allow yourself to be enveloped by the possibilities unfurling before you. What will you see? What will you feel in the depths of this new story?

Please write it down or stare at this empty page until it is filled with visions of magic, mystery and transformation.

Enjoy yourself!

52 THE SUSPICIOUS

Once upon a time, in a magical kingdom, there was a beautiful witch named Christina. She lived in a magnificent castle filled with magic and wonder, but she never left it. Christina was overcome with anxiety and suspicion, and she had become fearful of the outside world.

One day, as Christina was sitting in her castle, she was visited by three travelers. They were kind and curious, and they wanted to see the magic of Christina's castle. Christina was hesitant at first, but something about the travelers' kind demeanor and genuine curiosity made her feel comfortable.

As the travelers explored the castle, they marveled at the magic and wonder that Christina had created. They explored the enchanted gardens, gazed at the stars through the castle's magical telescope, and tasted the most delicious food and drinks.

As Christina watched the travelers enjoy her castle, she felt something stirring inside of her. For the first time in a long time, she felt a glimmer of hope and excitement. She realized that she had been missing out on all of the wonders of the world because of her fear and anxiety.

With the help of the travelers, Christina began to see the magic in the world again. She ventured outside of her castle and explored the nearby forests and meadows. She met new people and learned new things. She realized that the world was a beautiful and wondrous place and that there was so much to see and experience.

As Christina continued to explore the world, her anxiety, and suspicion began to fade away. She became more and more open to the magic of the world, and she learned to appreciate the beauty in everything. She realized that life was a gift and that every moment was precious.

And so, Christina continued to explore the world, experiencing all of its magic and wonder. She had learned to overcome her fears and anxieties, and she knew that she would never forget the lessons she had learned from the kind and curious travelers. She had found joy and wonder in the world, and she knew that she would always be grateful for the life she had been given.

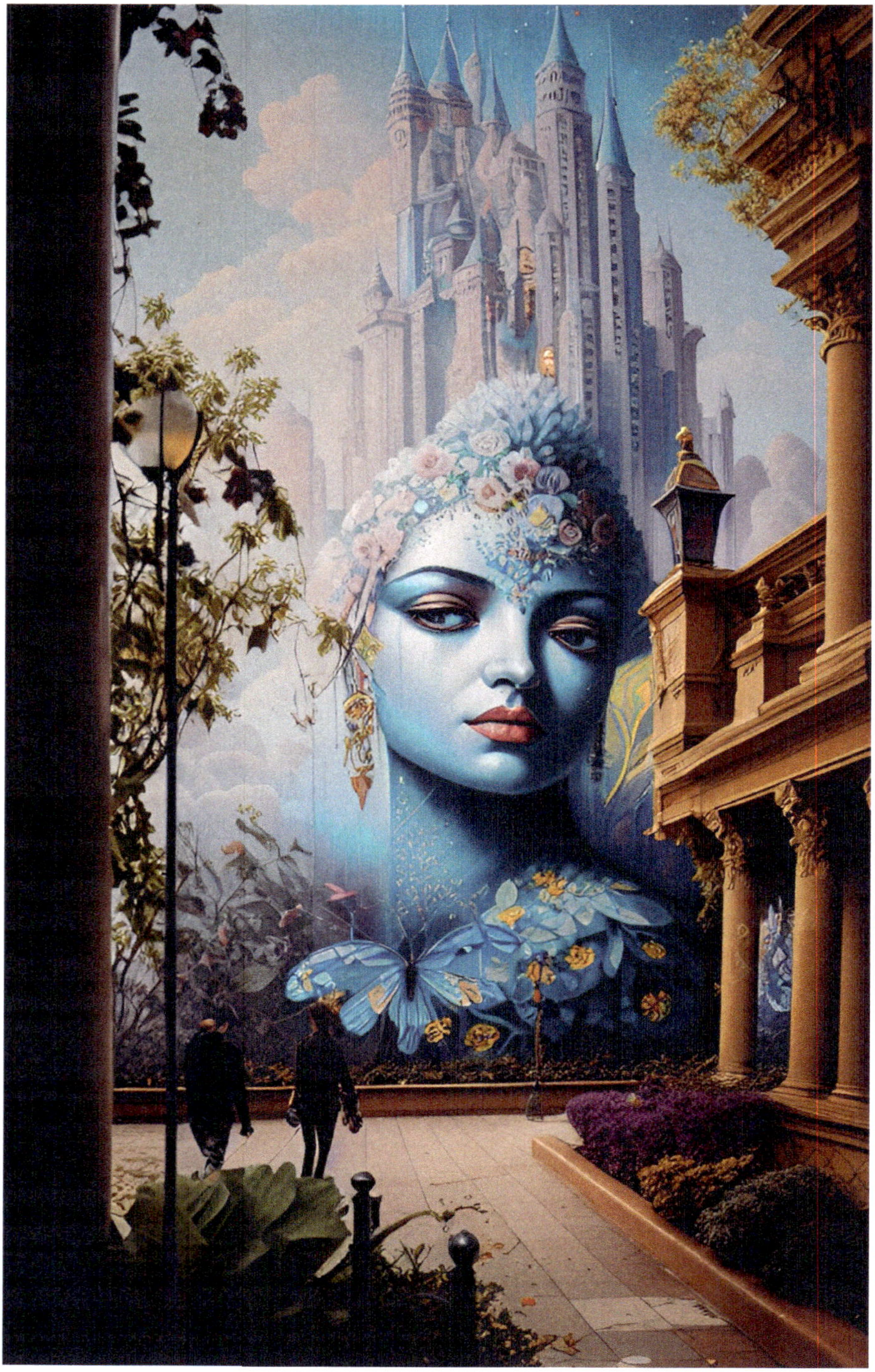

Close your eyes and still the time around you. Can you feel the story coming alive within you? What do you need to alter to create a new experience? Allow yourself to be enveloped by the possibilities unfurling before you. What will you see? What will you feel in the depths of this new story?

Please write it down or stare at this empty page until it is filled with visions of magic, mystery and transformation.

Enjoy yourself!

53 FORGOTTEN WAY INTO THE DREAM WORLD

Once upon a time, there was a beautiful, intelligent, and sensitive witch named Nina. She was gifted with magical powers and had a keen mind that allowed her to solve any problem. However, Nina had a major problem - she was very anxious and worried about everything. Her heart was so tormented and her mind so frayed that she even forgot her way to the dream world and stopped sleeping.

Nina lived in a small cottage on the edge of the woods. She spent most of her time alone, tending to her garden and practicing her magic. She was known throughout the land as the most talented witch but also as the most anxious one. She could never sit still and was always worrying about something.

One day, Nina's anxiety became too much for her to handle. She stopped sleeping and couldn't remember how to find her way to the dream world. She tried everything she could think of, but nothing worked. Her anxiety only grew worse, and she was afraid that she would never sleep again.

Desperate for a solution, Nina sought out the help of a wise old owl who lived deep in the woods. The owl had a reputation for being able to solve even the most challenging problems, and Nina hoped that he could help her.

The owl listened carefully to Nina's story and soon realized that her anxiety was the root of her problem. He advised her to practice mindfulness and meditation to calm her mind and reduce her stress.

At first, Nina was hesitant. She had always been an anxious person and didn't think that meditation would help her. But with the owl's guidance, she began to practice mindfulness and meditation every day.

Slowly but surely, Nina's anxiety began to fade. She was able to sleep again and found that her mind was clearer and more focused than ever before. She was able to channel her magical powers more effectively, and her spells became even more potent.

Nina continued to practice mindfulness and meditation, and soon she was able to conquer her anxiety once and for all. She was able to enjoy life to the fullest, and she became known throughout the land as the most talented and peaceful witch.

As Nina looked back on her journey, she realized that she had learned a valuable lesson. She had learned that sometimes, the greatest magic is found within oneself. By conquering her anxiety, she unlocked her full potential and became the best version of herself.

And so, Nina continued to live in her small cottage on the edge of the woods, using her magic to help those in need. She had found true peace and happiness, and she knew that she would always be grateful for the lessons she had learned on her journey.

MONETA AGENCY

Close your eyes and still the time around you. Can you feel the story coming alive within you? What do you need to alter to create a new experience? Allow yourself to be enveloped by the possibilities unfurling before you. What will you see? What will you feel in the depths of this new story?

Please write it down or stare at this empty page until it is filled with visions of magic, mystery and transformation.

Enjoy yourself!

54 THE MYSTERIOUS AND DECEPTIVE SIGNS

Once upon a time, in a magical kingdom, there lived a beautiful witch named Kali. Kali was known throughout the land for her unique ability to spot mysterious signs in the world around her. She would follow the signs wherever they led her, always eager to discover the secrets they held.

Kali's love for spotting signs started when she was just a young witch. One day, while wandering through the forest, she noticed a strange symbol etched into the bark of a tree. She followed the symbol deeper into the forest and soon found herself standing in front of a beautiful clearing. From that day on, Kali was hooked.

For many years, Kali followed signs all over the kingdom. She journeyed to distant lands and explored hidden places, always eager to discover the secrets that the signs held. She would spend days, and sometimes even weeks, following a single sign, determined to see where it would lead her.

But one day, something strange happened. Kali was following a sign that she had never seen before. It was a strange symbol that seemed to glow in the sunlight, beckoning her deeper into the forest. Kali followed the sign for hours until she realized that she was lost. The sign had led her deep into the heart of the forest, and she had no idea how to get back home.

For days, Kali wandered through the forest, searching for a way out. She was tired and hungry, and she missed her home terribly. She longed for her beautiful garden and the comfort of her castle. But no matter how hard she tried, she could not find her way home.

Finally, after many days of wandering, Kali stumbled upon a

small village. The people there were kind and welcoming, and they took Kali in and gave her food and shelter. Kali was grateful to the villagers for their kindness, but she longed to return to her home.

Over the years, Kali continued to follow mysterious signs, always searching for something new and exciting. But the signs seemed to be playing games with her, leading her farther and farther away from her home. Each time Kali followed a sign, she would get lost and end up in an unfamiliar area.

And each time Kali returned home, she found that her beautiful garden had fallen into disrepair. The flowers were wilted, and the plants were overgrown. Kali would have to start all over again, planting new flowers and tending to the garden until it was more beautiful.

For many years, Kali continued to follow mysterious signs, always eager to discover the secrets they held. She journeyed to distant lands and explored hidden places, always searching for something new and exciting. But no matter how hard she tried, she could never escape the games the signs played with her.

One day, as Kali was wandering through the forest, she came across a wise old owl. The owl looked at her with wise eyes, and Kali knew that he had something important to say.

"Dear Kali," said the owl, "you have been following mysterious signs for many years now. But the signs are not leading you where you want to go. They are taking you farther and farther away from your home, and you are losing everything that you hold dear. It is time for you to stop following the signs and start listening to your heart."

Kali was taken aback by the owl's words. She had never thought of it that way before. She had been so caught up in following the signs that she had forgotten about the truly important things to her.

And so, Kali took the owl's words to heart. She stopped following mysterious signs and started listening to her heart. She realized that what she truly wanted was to be at home.

55 WITCHES

Close your eyes and still the time around you. Can you feel the story coming alive within you? What do you need to alter to create a new experience? Allow yourself to be enveloped by the possibilities unfurling before you. What will you see? What will you feel in the depths of this new story?

Please write it down or stare at this empty page until it is filled with visions of magic, mystery and transformation.

Enjoy yourself!

55 THE CREATIVE

Once upon a time, in a magical kingdom, there lived a beautiful and clever witch named Elena. She was a master of many arts and crafts, and she loved nothing more than creating something new.

Elena's talent knew no bounds. She could sew the most beautiful dresses, paint the most stunning portraits, and cook the most delicious meals. She was always searching for something new to create, and her imagination was never-ending.

One day, Elena decided that she wanted to create something truly special. She had heard of a magical tree that was said to have the power to grant wishes, and she was determined to find it. So, she set out on a journey to discover the tree and create something truly unique.

Elena traveled through forests and over mountains for many days until she finally came to a clearing where the magical tree was said to grow. She stood before the tree in awe of its beauty and power, and she knew that she had found what she was looking for.

As she stood before the tree, Elena closed her eyes and made her wish. She wished for the power to create something truly unique, something that no one had ever seen before. And with a rustling of the leaves, the tree granted her wish.

Over the next few days, Elena worked tirelessly on her creation. She used all of her skills and talents to create something truly unique, something that would inspire and amaze anyone who saw it.

Finally, after many long hours of work, Elena's creation was complete. It was a dress unlike any other, made from the most beautiful and exotic materials. The colors were vibrant and stunning, and the design was intricate and elegant. It was a masterpiece, and Elena knew that she had truly created something special.

Elena decided to wear the dress to a grand ball, where all of the kingdom's most powerful and influential people would be in attendance. She knew that her creation would be the talk of the ball, and she was eager to show it off.

As she entered the ballroom, all eyes were on her. People gasped in amazement at the sight of her dress, and they marveled at the beauty of her creation. Everyone wanted to know who had made such a stunning dress, and Elena was proud to tell them that she had created it herself.

The night was a success, and Elena's creation was the talk of the town for weeks to come. People came from all over the kingdom to see her dress and marvel at the beauty of her creation. Elena was pleased with the success of her creation, but she knew that there was still more to be done.

She continued to create new and exciting things, always pushing herself to be better and more creative. She never lost her love for creating something new, and she knew that she would spend the rest of her days doing what she loved most.

And so, Elena continued to create, always seeking out new challenges and new adventures. She knew that the world was full of magic and wonder, and she was determined to discover it all. She had found her passion in life, and she knew that there was nothing that could stop her from creating something truly unique and amazing.

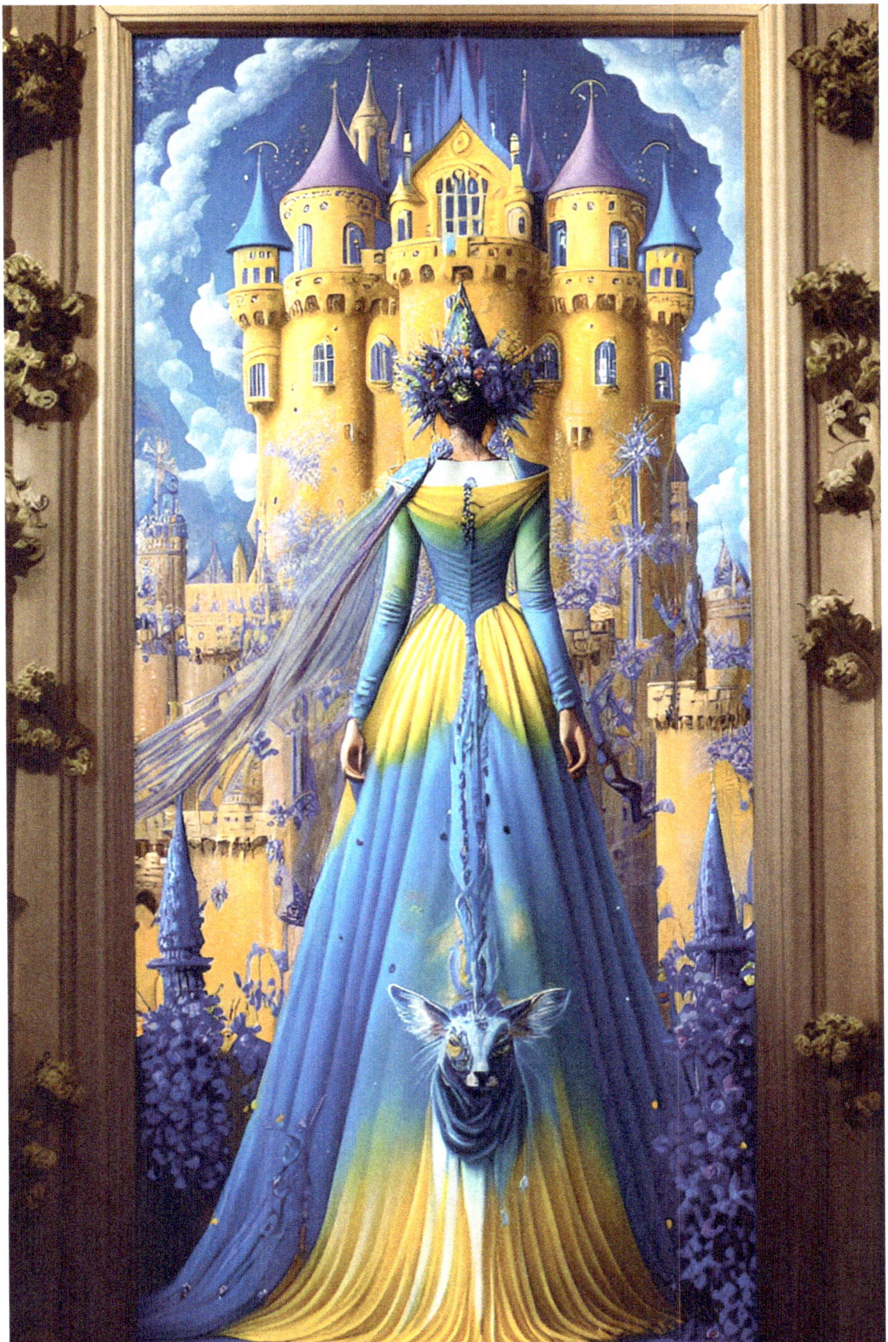

Close your eyes and still the time around you. Can you feel the story coming alive within you? What do you need to alter to create a new experience? Allow yourself to be enveloped by the possibilities unfurling before you. What will you see? What will you feel in the depths of this new story?

Please write it down or stare at this empty page until it is filled with visions of magic, mystery and transformation.

Enjoy yourself!

NO NUMBER STORY) THE UNIVERSAL DANCE

In the mystical land of Eldara, where magic flowed like the rivers and the air hummed with enchantment, there lived a beautiful, intelligent, and cheerful witch named Celestia. Celestia was known throughout Eldara for her unmatched magical prowess and her infectious joy. However, her life had not always been filled with such wonder and accomplishment.

In her early years, Celestia struggled to find her purpose and tap into the vast magical powers she knew lay dormant within her. She was often consumed by fear and doubt, which prevented her from reaching her full potential. She longed to uncover her higher purpose and to become a shining light for others in her community.

One day, while exploring a secluded grove deep within the enchanted forest, Celestia stumbled upon an ancient scroll, seemingly untouched by time. The scroll contained a series of proven techniques for manifesting one's purpose and overcoming fear. Eager to unlock her true potential, Celestia studied the scroll diligently, absorbing its wisdom and integrating its teachings into her daily life.

She learned to still her mind through meditation and focus her energy on her intentions, allowing her desires to flow effortlessly from her heart into the universe. As she practiced these techniques, Celestia began to uncover and embrace her innate magical talents. She realized that by aligning her thoughts and actions with the natural flow of the universe, she could achieve incredible mastery over her craft.

As Celestia's fears and doubts began to fade, she found herself more in tune with the universe and its boundless energy. She discovered her higher purpose: to guide and empower others on their own journeys of self-discovery and magical mastery. With her newfound clarity, Celestia dedicated herself to sharing her knowledge and helping others overcome their fears and limitations.

With each passing day, Celestia's mastery of the magical arts grew stronger, and her connection to the universe deepened. Her once-dim light now shone brightly, illuminating the lives of those around her. Her joy and enthusiasm for life were contagious, inspiring others to seek out their own paths and embrace the power within them.

As word of Celestia's teachings spread, witches and wizards from far and wide journeyed to Eldara to learn from her wisdom and experience the transformative power of manifesting one's purpose. Under Celestia's guidance, they too learned to overcome their fears and flow with the universe, unlocking their full potential and achieving their own magical mastery.

Celestia's influence reached far beyond the borders of Eldara, and her name became synonymous with the power of self-discovery and the magic of manifesting one's purpose. She became a shining light for all who sought to unlock their hidden talents and embrace their true potential.

And so, the beautiful, intelligent, and cheerful witch continued to share her light with the world, guiding others on their journeys and proving that, with the right tools and an unwavering belief in oneself, anyone can achieve incredible mastery and uncover their higher purpose.

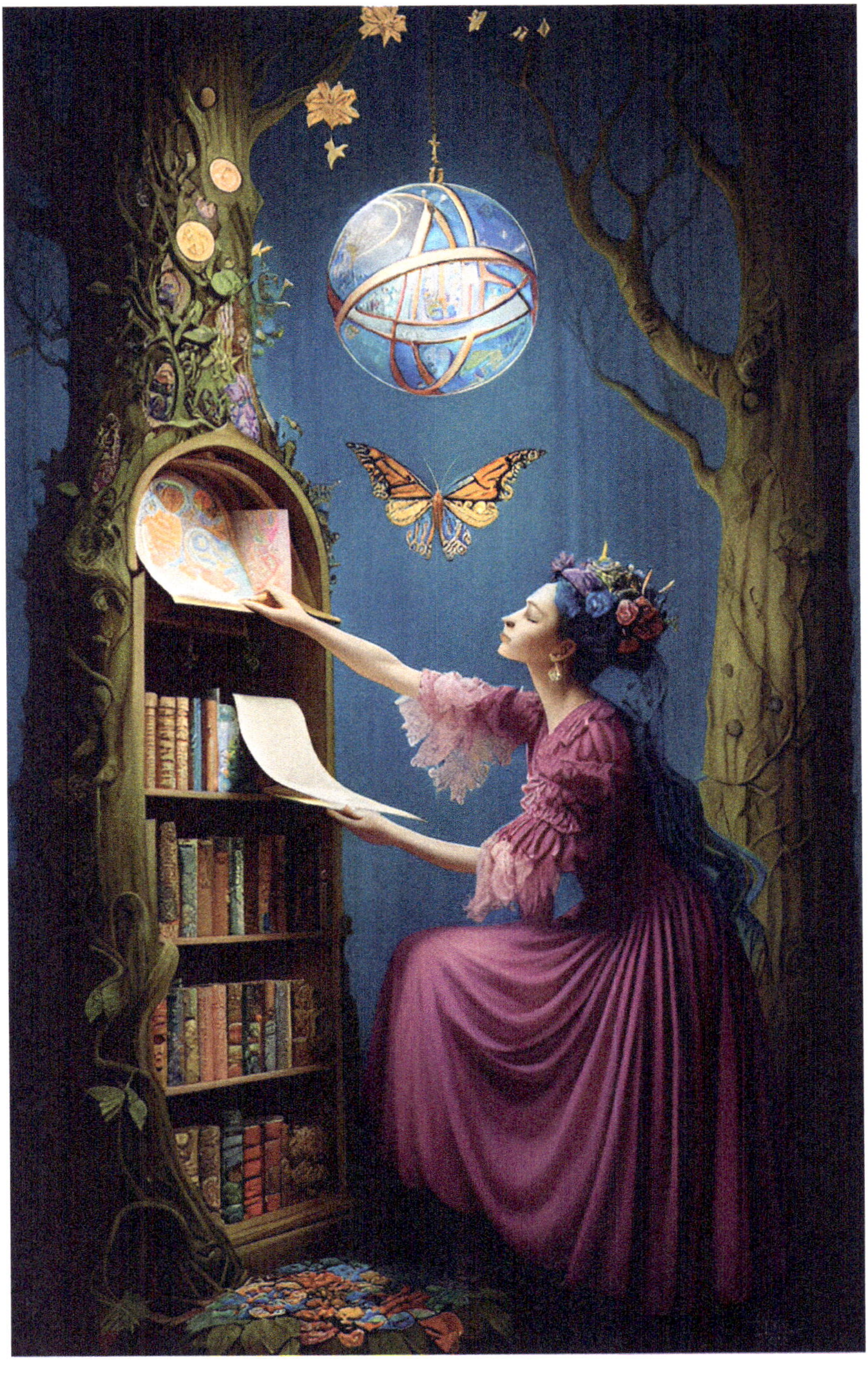

Close your eyes and still the time around you. Can you feel the story coming alive within you? What do you need to alter to create a new experience? Allow yourself to be enveloped by the possibilities unfurling before you. What will you see? What will you feel in the depths of this new story?

Please write it down or stare at this empty page until it is filled with visions of magic, mystery and transformation.

Enjoy yourself!

CONCLUSION

We sincerely hope that you enjoyed the stories. In conclusion, we have compiled for you another set of rules for the life of witches. They are wise and contradictory, just like life itself.

Witches have no regrets - Witches understand that the past is in the past and cannot be changed, so they live each day believing that whatever happened was meant to happen and everything will be as it should be.

Witches Make Mistakes - Witches recognize that they may make mistakes or misjudge a situation from time to time, and they are willing to learn from their mistakes. They do not take failure or criticism as a personal attack but use what they have learned to become wiser and to know themselves and the world around them better.

Witches make jokes - Although witches are powerful beings, they also understand the importance of having fun. Whether it's pranking each other or engaging in recreational activities such as gardening or photography, witches often find ways to enjoy life while staying connected to their craft.

Witches Know Yourself - It is important for witches to be self-aware and honest with themselves about their feelings, thoughts, and intentions in order to remain true to their path as spiritual beings. By deepening this connection with themselves, witches better understand how they can use their innate knowledge and abilities to benefit the world.

Witches Understand People - Through careful observation and empathy, witches can pick up on subtle signals from others that reveal unspoken truths behind conversations or behaviors and determine whether or not a person's intentions toward them are sincere.

Witches Learn from Nature - Nature is a clever teacher, revealing secrets through her cycles and energies that bind us all together as part of something greater than ourselves. Understanding how nature works help witches gain a deeper understanding of magic and its potential power in our lives when used properly.

Witches Expect Miracles from the Future - Wise witches know that while we cannot always control what happens in our lives, there are still moments when we get glimpses into a world beyond our own lives where anything is possible if we only believe it can be true.

Witches Live in the Moment - For some witches, embracing the "here and now" provides comfort in difficult times because being aware of current circumstances allows us to appreciate each moment for what it brings rather than worrying about what could go wrong.

Witches Don't Worry About Anything - Finally, wise witches know how much energy is wasted on unnecessary worries, so they focus on looking positively at a situation rather than letting negative thoughts consume them.

Witches don't hope for anything - Witches understand that expectations can lead to disappointment, so they focus on cultivating contentment, knowing that things will always end up the way they were intended.

Witches Expect Nothing - Instead of looking outside themselves for answers, witches know that they need to look inside themselves to find inner strength and understanding in their path.

Witches want for nothing - Instead of wanting or needing something from others, witches trust and believe in themselves and their own abilities, which leads them down the path of self-improvement and liberation.

Witches don't need anything-they don't rely on outside forces or material possessions to make themselves happy, as this only leads to greater levels of dissatisfaction over time because of our inability to control these things.

Witches are always confident - Knowing who you are and what you are worth is important to any witch because it helps build confidence, which allows them to make decisions without hesitation or fear of failure.

Witches love themselves - Self-love is essential if one wants to develop a strong connection to their craft, as this type of unconditional self-acceptance creates an even deeper level of trust between the witch and her intuition.

Witches are people who are always capable of being successful - For many witches, success requires not only the ability but also stamina, determination, risk-taking skills, and creativity. With all of these qualities combined with magical abilities, witches often create powerful spells and rituals that lead to positive changes in the world.

Witches believe in themselves - maintaining a positive attitude even when faced with difficult challenges gives witches an advantage over those who fear failure or loss of hope. Believing in ourselves will help make any idea a reality, rather than succumbing to negative thinking patterns that can keep us from fulfilling our dreams.

Witches are always prepared for the future anyway-the knowledge that life can take an unexpected turn at any moment helps witches be prepared for what comes next. As a result, they remain adaptable, learning new skills and keeping an open mind to any life changes, so they can easily deal with any surprises that come their way.

Witches are always prepared for any situation - Experience with different kinds of magic gives witches a greater understanding of how combinations of spells work together, making it easier for them to think quickly in unexpected situations.

Witches are creators of their own destiny - Through dedication and practice, witches gain power over fate and chance, aligning magical energies with intention so that they can manifest specific results through spells based on personal goals.

Witches are always calm - Through meditative practice and introspection, witches cultivate inner peace when faced with external chaos, so they can remain focused on the task at hand with rational thought.

Witches are always optimistic - Knowing that no matter how difficult something may seem, there is always an opportunity to learn and grow helps witches stay hopeful, believing that better times are ahead, no matter what life throws their way.

Witches don't get lost in the woods - Using their knowledge of the elements and being aware of their surroundings, witches don't succumb to fear or confusion when out in nature but use it as a place to reconnect with themselves and the world around them.

Witches don't let other people run their lives - It is important for any witch to feel comfortable in their own skin to remember that personal freedom is something that cannot be taken away as long as they believe in who they are.

Witches don't allow other people into their lives - Experienced witches know that it's important to pay attention to who you allow inside your circle because those closest to us often influence our craft more than we think. For this reason, they set clear boundaries between themselves and those who try to manipulate or abuse their power for self-serving purposes.

Witches Don't Tolerate Stupidity - Despite their open minds, witches also understand when to be firm about things that are inconsistent with who they are or what they stand for. They reject anything that contradicts their beliefs but remains compassionate toward others, even if they disagree.

Witches don't wait for someone else to take the initiative - Instead of depending on someone else, wise witches understand the importance of leading by example themselves by taking the first steps toward creating change in their communities or solving global problems.

The witches go on living - Even in dark times, witches never give up because there is always a tomorrow waiting for us after every night that passes. Knowing that life never stays the same, no matter how hard things get, helps witches keep moving forward with courage and determination, no matter what obstacles get in their way.

Witches are creators. With creativity comes power. That is, everything that manifests itself in art, music, writing, etc., can shape reality. Wise witches understand the impact these forms of expression can have on our lives, so they use them daily as they continue to embrace new ideas and perspectives.

Witches take full responsibility for their lives-they understand that the choices they make directly affect the outcome of their situations, so they strive to live consciously and honestly in order to achieve the best results.

Witches are friends with people who are better than they are - Knowing that it takes more than magic to create a beautiful life, witches surround themselves with those who have different skills as well as similar interests - because together, they can bring out the best in each other and create something truly beautiful.

Witches know how to respect themselves - Taking the time to take care of yourself and prioritize your needs is essential for any witch. After all, if you don't fill your own cup first, how can you expect others to? This is why witches put themselves first and show true appreciation for what makes them unique.

Witches know how to respect others - Just as it is important to respect yourself, it is also important to respect everyone around you. Recognizing that all living beings are composed of the same essence is part of being a witch, which means understanding and honoring each person's individual path without placing judgment or expectations on that path.

Witches know how to take risks - Taking calculated risks is natural for witches because they know that sometimes failure is part of learning. By having the courage to make difficult decisions, these brave souls set an example for others by showing them that it is possible to be brave, no matter what the outcome may be.

Witches know how to respect themselves - Learning to love yourself from within lays a solid foundation from which personal growth begins. Self-respect means recognizing one's worth regardless of outside opinions or circumstances, which allows a witch to be more self-confident when faced with difficulties along the way.

Witches know how to respect their bodies - taking care of their physicality is key for any witch because it serves as a reminder that we are all connected to the Earth, and our health depends on what we put into our being. For this reason, witches seek to fill their days with nourishment, not neglect, in order to remain alert and energetic.

Witches are in tune with themselves - Belief in oneself is very important to any witch, and this begins with finding a balance between body and mind by turning inward rather than endlessly searching outside oneself. This, in turn, fuels a sense of acceptance and also builds confidence in oneself, equipping witches with the inner wisdom they need in their spiritual quest.

Witches do not inflict pain - Caring for others is natural for many witches, who go to great lengths to refrain from inflicting pain on others out of respect for life. Violence is not tolerated because it will only create more disharmony in a worldview already fractured by suffering.

Witches don't steal - Possessions are meaningless when juxtaposed with principles such as loyalty, justice, and fair play, which are more important values that magical beings swear by. Therefore, no matter how advantageous the situation may seem at first glance, stealing will never be justified according to a witch's value system.

Witches do not kill - Life is sacred in witch culture; this means that all living things will be spared if possible unless raiding parties or rival forces threaten the safety of communities when they have no choice but to engage in hostilities. Regardless of the circumstances, witches still take precautions, such as praying for the souls of victims before engaging in combat and never taking another's life lightly or without warning.

.Witches do not coerce - Coercion brings nothing but harm and chaos to anyone, which most witches try to avoid whenever possible. Rather than demanding obedience from another person or creature, wise witches learn to use methods of persuasion, such as negotiation, when necessary to ensure that both parties reach a mutual agreement in any conflict that arises.

Witches Don't Shrink - Knowing the value of resources, experienced witches understand that depriving others, while they have plenty of them, can ultimately lead to ruin. Therefore, the few true witches selfishly accumulate things solely for their own benefit when faced with a situation of scarcity but instead share whatever they can provide with those who need it.

Witches do not abuse-whether physically or emotionally-exploiting someone's trust is not something firmly rooted in witch culture because it goes against everything that nature stands for, namely, treating everyone equally, regardless of the circumstances surrounding them. As a result, young people learn early on the consequences to which abusive behavior can lead, so it is rarely seen in magical societies.

Witches Don't Forget Who They Are - It's easy to get lost in society's many expectations of acceptable behavior, but the wise are always mindful of their true selves, hidden beneath all social norms. While this does not mean that following the rules is irrelevant, honoring one's own individuality helps keep the inner compass on a straight path, even during the worst storms.

Witches don't catch up with others - Competition with other people or groups is not what witches do, as it only creates disharmony and discord instead of promoting understanding and cooperation. Instead, they strive to remain true to themselves, living up to their values and setting boundaries of what is acceptable and unacceptable. This allows them to develop at their own pace without the pressure of having to "catch up" with others.

Witches are not afraid of loneliness - Loneliness is often perceived as something negative, but many witches understand that it can be a source of comfort. They use this feeling to turn within themselves and explore themselves, which allows them to process the events of their lives and gain insight into the future. In this way, they can enjoy solitude and find beauty in the present moment.

Witches are not afraid of silence - Silence is considered a powerful tool in witchcraft because it gives practitioners time for reflection and clarity. Those who practice it gain power through silence, learning to accept both peaceful and difficult moments calmly, without judgment or expectation.

Witches do not fear death - Death is not something to fear in witchcraft, for life is cyclical; what has been lost will come again. One day, when their own time comes, wise witches will face death with courage, knowing that all life eventually returns back to nature, which never stops its healing process, no matter how grim things may seem.

Witches are not afraid of themselves - Self-love is a key element of witchcraft, so witches learn early on that fear is useless. Nevertheless, even the highest-ranking witches can sometimes succumb to negative thoughts, but they try to quickly replace them with positive affirmations of the power contained within.

Witches are not afraid of nature - nature itself is of great importance to magical beings, as it is where most spells take place because of the abundance of resources provided there, as well as the residence of other spirits. For these reasons, few among those of this craft ever take refuge in the wildest places but instead boldly go out in search of guidance from those there.

Witches are not afraid of animals-the hallmark of the practice of the true witch is the reverence for creatures large and small, whether they are traditionally considered "dangerous" or "friendly" by society's standards. As a result, it is rare to find someone who avoids contact with animals even in times of fear, but rather who befriends random creatures, showing them respect, since we all live on the same Earth.

Witches Don't Give Up - True witches never stop fighting

for what they believe in; they understand that every effort counts, no matter how insignificant it may seem at first glance. After each setback, practitioners regroup, focus their energy on what lies ahead, and keep going, even though they face more challenges than others can endure in a lifetime.

Witches don't lose faith - Faith plays an important role in witchcraft, as belief systems provide much-needed support during the intense struggle. Regardless of the harsh conditions they face, the faithful retain the spirit of nurture within them to defeat the long odds stacked against them, often realizing the dreams they hold most dear.

Witches don't stop at the first failure - If something doesn't work the first time, so be it; persistent souls simply pick themselves up, gather themselves up, and try again with renewed vigor until they achieve the desired result. Regardless of the daunting task or heartbreaking situation they face, true witches will persevere to the very end, even if it takes several attempts over a period of time to achieve the goals set originally.

Witches are not oblivious to who they are - not only aware of their capabilities but also aware of the deep connection between humans and the world around them; "true" witches are not easily led astray by the erroneous influences of external forces that elude the personality they hold sacred. For this reason alone, always remember who is really behind the mask you put on daily, even though you sometimes go astray.

Witches are not afraid of the unknown - True witches understand the power of accepting uncertainty and remaining open to whatever may come. Instead of resisting, they accept that life holds surprises and find ways to make the most of any situation. This allows them to overcome any obstacle without hesitation or trepidation.

Witches are not afraid of the future - practitioners of witchcraft recognize that while life is unpredictable, the future is always filled with hope and possibility. They trust the events that unfold before them, knowing that everything that happens can be used as an opportunity for growth and self-development with the right approach.

Witches Don't Resist What Happens - Acceptance of change is a basic principle of witchcraft; rather than fighting it, wise witches accept it with open arms and use it as a chance to learn more about themselves and grow as individuals. They may even choose to turn any failure into a positive experience, finding creative ways to adapt their behavior so as not to be consumed by the events unfolding around them.

Witches don't try to change the past - dwelling on what has been can't change what lies ahead, so practitioners usually focus on how they can use past experiences productively rather than trying uselessly to change themselves or the environment that has already happened. This allows them to see the future better without needlessly wasting energy on regrets that can never return to the present moment.

Witches don't wait for help - Taking matters into one's own hands instead of asking others for help is the hallmark of a true witch's practice since everyone is responsible for their own destiny, regardless of the presence or absence of physical disabilities. Those who thrive in this craft fully understand the value of self-sufficiency, so they seek to live independently and confidently whenever possible.

Witches don't think about what could go wrong - Fear is not something typically common among members of this magical community, as thinking about "what if" scenarios usually distracts from achieving goals. On the contrary, most prefer positive thinking, turning ideas into reality through determination stored in connected, powerful belief systems, ready to unleash.

Witches don't like to reflect on their past - Reflection is certainly an important aspect of a witch's journey, but remembering situations that constantly arise can hinder further progress because of a focus on failures and mistakes made over time. Therefore, while some introspection is necessary in order to process emotions properly, it is equally important to avoid getting stuck by wallowing in all the pitfalls encountered previously.

Witches do not judge others - Showing compassionate understanding when considering decisions made are arranged ways of walking belong to fellow human beings common courtesy displayed by many societies accepting differences between people despite ideologies followed by religions adhered to. As a result, true practices treat everyone with equal respect. Ideally, as much humanity deserves, even those who despise openly questioned publicly.

LEAVE THE REWIEV

As an agency striving to bring independent authors' works to the public, reviews are vital for us to gauge the success of our efforts. If you enjoyed this book and want to help us continue producing quality stories, please express your opinion by writing a review. Reviews are the lifeblood of this platform, often the first step potential readers take when looking for new titles. Your honest review will be invaluable.

We appreciate your support and look forward to hearing from you soon

Printed in Great Britain
by Amazon